P9-DOB-979

Beatrix Potter Collectibles

The Peter Rabbit Story Characters

Debby DuBay and Kara Sewall

Photography by Linda LaBonte-Britt & Kindra Clineff

Schiffer Publishing Ltd

4880 Lower Valley Road, Atglen, PA 19310 USA

Dedication

This book is dedicated to all who have been comforted in life by Peter Rabbit or other of Beatrix Potter's characters, and to John and Kara Sewall who have dedicated their lives to collecting them.

Library of Congress Cataloging-in-Publication Data

DuBay, Debby.
  Beatrix Potter collectibles : the Peter Rabbit story characters / Debby DuBay and Kara Sewall.
      p. cm.
  ISBN 0-7643-2358-X (pbk.)
  1. Potter, Beatrix, 1866-1943—Characters—Collectibles. 2. Peter Rabbit (Fictitious character) in art. I. Sewall, Kara. II. Title.

NK928.D83 2006
823'.912—dc22
                                                                    2005025370

Copyright © 2006 by Debby DuBay & Kara Sewall

    All rights reserved. No part of this work may be reproduced or used in any form or by any means—graphic, electronic, or mechanical, including photocopying or information storage and retrieval systems—without written permission from the publisher.
    The scanning, uploading and distribution of this book or any part thereof via the Internet or via any other means without the permission of the publisher is illegal and punishable by law. Please purchase only authorized editions and do not participate in or encourage the electronic piracy of copyrighted materials.
    "Schiffer," "Schiffer Publishing Ltd. & Design," and the "Design of pen and ink well" are registered trademarks of Schiffer Publishing Ltd.

Designed by Mark David Bowyer
Type set in Geometr231 Hv BT / Souvenir Lt BT

ISBN: 0-7643-2358-X
Printed in China
1 2 3 4

Published by Schiffer Publishing Ltd.
4880 Lower Valley Road
Atglen, PA 19310
Phone: (610) 593-1777; Fax: (610) 593-2002
E-mail: Info@schifferbooks.com

For the largest selection of fine reference books on this and related subjects, please visit our web site at
www.schifferbooks.com
We are always looking for people to write books on new and related subjects. If you have an idea for a book please contact us at the above address.

This book may be purchased from the publisher.
Include $3.95 for shipping.
Please try your bookstore first.
You may write for a free catalog.

In Europe, Schiffer books are distributed by
Bushwood Books
6 Marksbury Ave.
Kew Gardens
Surrey TW9 4JF England
Phone: 44 (0) 20 8392-8585; Fax: 44 (0) 20 8392-9876
E-mail: info@bushwoodbooks.co.uk
Free postage in the U.K., Europe; air mail at cost.

Contents

Once upon a time there were four little Rabbits, and their names were- Flopsy, Mopsy, Cotton tail, and Peter.

Foreword

Little did Beatrix Potter imagine when she made her Peter Rabbit doll in 1903 that over a century later a book would be published in the United States of America about her "collectibles." Commercial products based on children's books were not a new idea in England even in Beatrix's time, the tradition having been started at least two hundred years earlier. But Beatrix Potter had a good commercial eye and when she saw that products closely associated with characters from her books were starting to appear in the shops in London, she took the matter into her own hands. Her Peter Rabbit doll she made - and registered at the Patent Office - on December 28, 1903. She then gave the doll to her editor for his niece, warning him that, 'I have not got it right yet, but the expression is going to be lovely…I think I could make him stand on his legs if he had some lead bullets in his feet!' It was the start of what Beatrix was later to call, "All the little side shows."

For over seventeen years Kara Sewall has been the eyes and ears for the many collectors of Beatrix Potter merchandise all over the world. They write to her at first for information and identification of their Potter collectibles but very soon they are proud to call her their friend. This record of Beatrix Potter collectibles by Kara and Debby DuBay is unique and there is little doubt that it will stand for many years as a valuable reference book for all of us.

Judy Taylor
author and authority
on Beatrix Potter

Introduction and Acknowledgments

Beatrix Potter's famous Peter Rabbit first made his appearance in a picture letter written to a sick child in 1893. Since then the Tales have become an essential part of English childhood, and, over the years, have captivated both adults and children alike. I thought I had stepped back in time to 1893 when I first visited the "mouse house" of Kara and John Sewall in the historic town of Andover, Massachusetts.

Oddly enough, I met Kara Sewall through a little English woman who frequented my Limoges Antique Shop in downtown Andover, Massachusetts. Wensley so wanted Kara and me to meet, but due to an early adult onset of Multiple Sclerosis (MS), Kara has been basically home and wheel chair bound since 1985. I decided to make a visit to this mouse house and meet Kara Sewall. I will always remember my first visit to Kara's. There she was sitting on her deck, in her wheel chair, with live chipmunks literally running across her feet and legs! Beatrix Potter characters littered her deck, wind chimes of Peter Rabbit and his friends chirped in the wind, and then there was her garden: an enchanted place with Beatrix Potter characters, each hand crafted and carved by her husband, John, and given to her on Christmas mornings. I was captivated by what I saw: Peter Rabbit in Mr. McGregor's garden, Peter Rabbit running under that infamous gate, Peter Rabbit and the watering can, and Peter Rabbit and the scarecrow. No detail is too small for the Sewall's garden and looking closer I saw Mr. McGregor's spade (with a friendly Robin perched on its handle), wheel barrel, and sieve. Fierce Bad Rabbit sitting on a bench and a ivy topiary of Tom Kitten are nestled among the scenic woodsy background of this lovely New England home. I was smitten by the scene, and if one didn't have the love of Beatrix Potter at that point—well, I still had not stepped inside the mouse house!

Peter Rabbit book and a collection of four Peter Rabbits by Eden.

Once inside, I was overwhelmed by the massive collection of Beatrix Potter. Hundreds of Schmid music boxes and ornaments litter her entryway. Schmid flat ceramic ornaments hang on her wall like a border. Schmid Concept Villages are lit up by Schmid night lights. Eden plush toys of every Beatrix Potter character in all sizes are encased or sit on tiny antique pieces of furniture. Hundreds of pieces of Wedgwood Nursery Ware are displayed in antique oak display cases and several hundred beautiful enameled Crummles boxes are in tiny wooden cases hanging on her walls. Not to mention the hundreds of tiny collections stuffed in cabinets and behind closed doors that I have now had the privilege to peek at!

It has been ten years since my love affair with Kara Sewall, Beatrix Potter, and Peter Rabbit and his friends began. Kara's love encompasses almost two decades and many have fallen in love with Kara and her overwhelming enthusiasm, knowledge, and collection of Beatrix Potter: Judy Taylor, author and authority on Beatrix Potter, whom we sincerely thank for setting the tone of our book with her lovely foreword; Hilary Wheeler, past Beatrix Potter Society Newsletter editor; Mary Fry, owner, Rose Tree Cottage Tea House that serves the royal families when visiting the United States; and Nora C. Swenson who contributed her research on Beatrix Potter figurines and allowed us to include pieces from her private collection.

I am honored that Kara has allowed me to document her fantastic collection and extensive knowledge of Beatrix Potter. The research of the items photographed in this book took years by expert and long time collector Kara Sewall. And, I am grateful to my long time publishing company Schiffer Publishing Ltd.—specifically Nancy Schiffer, who enabled us to accomplish our goal: to expose readers to the charming characters loved by Beatrix Potter so that collectors, young and old, will continue to be comforted by Peter Rabbit and his friends.

Debby DuBay, Ret, USAF, AAA

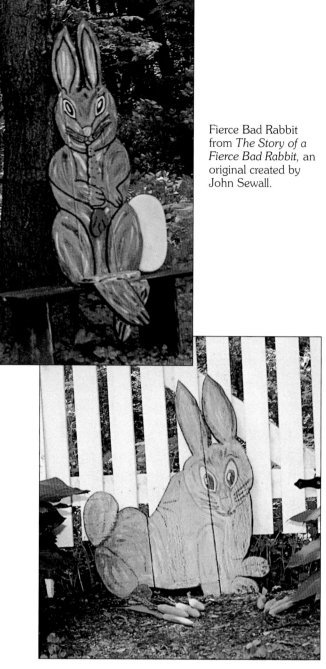

Fierce Bad Rabbit from *The Story of a Fierce Bad Rabbit,* an original created by John Sewall.

Peter Rabbit from *The Tale of Peter Rabbit* going under the gate at the "Mouse House," an original created by John Sewall.

Peter Rabbit and the watering can from *The Tale of Peter Rabbit,* an original created by John Sewall.

Mr. McGregor's scarecrow from *The Tale of Peter Rabbit*, an original created by John Sewall.

Mr. McGregor's wheel barrow from *The Tale of Peter Rabbit*, an original created by John Sewall.

Beatrix Potter

1984 Wedgwood Commemorative Beatrix Potter Plate. 1000 plates produced exclusively for the National Trust. The 10" bone china plate features an illustration of Beatrix Potter, hat in hand, surrounded by sheep, looking down on the village of Sawrey. $350.

Say the name Beatrix Potter and simple animals of the English countryside come to life: Peter Rabbit, Jemima Puddle-duck, Tom Kitten, and Pigling Bland. Beatrix Potter's fascination with her childhood pets and her ability to make each take on life-like characteristics make her stories beloved by children of all ages. More than a writer of nursery tales, Beatrix Potter was a farmer and landowner, a breeder and judge of award winning Herdwick sheep, and one of the great benefactors of the National Trust in England.

Helen Beatrix Potter was born on 28 July, 1866, in South Kensington, London, to affluent parents during the Victorian Era. Beatrix and her younger brother, Bertram, lived their childhood in the third floor nursery of Number 2 Bolton Gardens. Their parents rarely went upstairs to see them, and only on occasion would have them brought down into the main parlor for inspection or to take them to one of the various Unitarian churches that the Potters attended.

Beatrix never attended schools like her brother, but was taught at home by a strict Scottish nurse and a succession of governesses, her favorite being a young woman named Annie Carter. As a young child living in London, Beatrix Potter was fascinated by nature. With her younger brother Bertram, she collected animals, skeletons and fossils. The upstairs nursery became home to an assortment of pets, such as rabbits, mice, and toads. Beatrix and Bertram studied, drew, and painted pictures of plants and animals that they kept as pets. When allowed out of the house, the two would spend hours at the Natural History Museum to study and sketch insects, fossils, and stuffed animals. Beatrix Potter's drawings of mushrooms were beautiful and accurate in every detail, but—being a young girl during the Victorian Era—the museum overlooked her talent. However, in 1967, almost seventy years after they were originally drawn, fifty-nine of her watercolor paintings appeared in a book about British mushrooms called *Wayside & Woodland Fungi*, by W. P. K. Findlay.

For many years as a child, Beatrix Potter's parents took the children on three-month, summer holidays to Scotland, giving them plenty of time to sketch and do watercolors of caterpillars, flowers, and scenery. When Beatrix was 16, the house they rented became unavailable so they rented Wray Castle, near Ambleside in England's Lake District. Her parents entertained many prominent guests of Lakeland, including Hardwicke Rawnsley, vicar of Wray Church, who, in 1895, became one of the original founders of the National Trust. Their views on the need to preserve the natural beauty of the Lake District had a lasting effect on the young Beatrix, who had fallen in love with the unspoiled beauty surrounding their holiday home. Traveling around the country with her parents added first-hand experience, and it is this deep love and knowledge of the Lake District countryside that later became so apparent in her books.

Over the next two decades, the Potters vacationed in the Lake District, staying once at Wray Castle, once at Fawe Park, twice at Holehird, and nine times at Lingholm, by Derwentwater, famous now for its rhododendron gardens. Beatrix loved Derwentwater, and explored Catbells behind Lingholm. She watched squirrels in the woods, saw rabbits in the vegetable gardens of the big house and made many sketches of the animals and the landscape. (Her book *The Tale of Squirrel Nutkin* has

A wonderful collection of hand made Beatrix Potter and characters. Beatrix Potter is on the far left. $100.

background views based on Derwentwater, Catbells and the Newlands Valley; Fawe Park was featured in *The Tale of Benjamin Bunny*.) The Potters kept in touch with Reverend Rawnsley who, after five years at Wray, moved to Crosthwaite Church just outside Keswick.

In 1880, when Beatrix was 15, she started writing a secret journal. This journal was not a diary about her, but a book written in extremely tiny code on current events, her father's moods, and the every day life of the era. The journal ended in 1895 when she was thirty years old. A cousin discovered it in a bureau at Castle Cottage in 1952, almost a decade after Beatrix Potter's death. Mr. Leslie Linder, an avid collector of Beatrix paintings and sketches, labored for nine years to transcribe the 200,000 word diary and it was published in 1966, the centenary of her birth, as the *Journal of Beatrix Potter*.

After Bertram began boarding away at school, his sister was allowed drawing lessons and at age 17 she was allowed twelve lessons in painting. Later, she stated that her greatest regret was that she never studied anatomy or learned to draw the human figure. Reverend Rawnsley continued to visit the Potters and encouraged Beatrix to draw. When back in London Beatrix made greetings cards of her pictures and in 1890 she sent six designs for Christmas cards to the German firm of Hildesheimer & Faulkner. She was paid handsomely for her first published works. On September 4, 1893, Beatrix wrote an eight-page letter to an ill child, five year old Noel Moore, the oldest child of her favorite former governess, Annie Carter. Annie had married and become the mother of eight children, the youngest named Beatrix. The letter to Noel was a tale about a rabbit named Peter. Having success with her cards and calendars, Beatrix decided to try to have her story about Peter professionally published. Seven years after having sent Noel Moore his famous letter, she asked to borrow it, made a few revisions, created more sketches, and set about getting her book published. In 1901, after sending it to six publishers, including Frederick Warne & Company, and receiving six rejection letters, she decided to publish it privately. Beatrix published 250 editions and specified that the book was to measure 5 inches by 3 ¾ inches, making it easier for little hands to hold. (Today her books measure 5 inches by 4 inches.) She also insisted that a sketch appear every time a page was turned. She gave away her books to friends and relatives, and in two weeks had 200 more books published.

Mr. Rawnsley, now a founder of the National Trust, encouraged Beatrix to publish her book. He submitted it again to Frederick Warne & Company, who this time agreed to publish it if Beatrix would prepare colored illustrations throughout. In 1902 *The Tale of Peter Rabbit* was published. *The Tale of Peter Rabbit* was the prototype for the first of all the tales, beginning with the famous list of names: Flopsy, Mopsy, Cottontail and Peter. The original Peter Rabbit was Beatrix Potter's beloved pet Belgium rabbit, who drank out of toy teacups and slept in front of the fireplace on an old quilt made of blue flannel cloth. When he died in 1901, Beatrix wrote in her personal copy of the story, "Dedicated to an affectionate companion and quiet friend." Today *The Tale of Peter Rabbit* is known as the best-selling children's classic of all time; well over forty million copies have been sold. It has never been out of print and is available in over thirty-five foreign languages, in Braille, record, compact disc, and digital videodisc formats.

With income from the sale of her book, Beatrix bought a field in Near Sawrey in 1903, close to the area where she and her family had vacationed that year. By 1905, over 50,000 copies of *The Tale of Peter Rabbit* had sold, and it was that year she bought Hill Top, a tiny, 17th century, rambling and unkempt farm in Sawrey. Beatrix still lived at home in London with her parents, but she hired John Cannon, accompanied by his wife and two children, to live in her little house and to farm her land. For the next eight years, Beatrix busied herself writing more books and visiting her farm. During this time she wrote *The Pie and The Patty-Pan*, *The Tale of Jeremy Fisher,* and *The Tale of Tom Kitten. Jemima Puddle-duck* was about a real duck that lived at Hill Top and the drawings are of her farm; it is dedicated to the children of the Cannon family who worked it. Her book *The Tale of Pigling Bland* contained sketches of her own pigs as well as a rare self-portrait.

Seven of her books are based in or around Hill Top. Tom Kitten and Samuel Whiskers lived there, and at any moment one might expect to catch a glimpse of Tom Kitten in a doorway, or Jemima Puddle-duck splashing in the garden pond. Hill Top was never lived in by Beatrix for long periods of time but used to house her antiques, books and sketches. It is still as it was then, and is now the most visited literary shrine in the Lake District.

In 1909 she bought another farm, Castle Farm, which was near Hill Top and became her main Lakeland vacation home. During the purchase negotiations she met William Heelis, a solicitor in Hawkshead. They were married in 1913 and stayed in a furnished bungalow until Castle Cottage, the home on the property, was renovated. (The office of William Heelis is now the National Trust's Beatrix Potter Gallery.) With her marriage came the end of Beatrix's creative writing period. Six more books were published, *The Tale of Johnny Town-Mouse* being the only one with the style and spirit of her earlier works.

Beatrix Potter's love and knowledge of animals developed into a passionate interest in becoming a farmer. With her marriage and move to Castle Cottage, the next stage of her life began: that of a Lakeland farmer. Beatrix Potter bred prize pigs (one of which became immortalized as Pigling Bland), but she is better known for her expert breeding of Herdwick sheep.

A wonderful hand made Beatrix Potter Doll c.1995. The creator has painstakingly created details in order that this doll portrays an accurate representation of the real Beatrix Potter. $100.

In 1923, at the age of 57, Beatrix purchased Troutbeck Park Farm, where she devoted herself to breeding Herdwick sheep, a tough native sheep of the Lake District noted for its hard waterproof wool used in the making of carpets. Mrs. Heelis was becoming one of the most respected farmers in the Lake County where she was known as a breeder and judge of Herdwick sheep. In 1930 she became the first woman president of the Herdwick Sheepbreeders Association. This accomplishment was based on respect for her ability as a farmer — as few knew about her books, much less would they have considered them important to breeding sheep. Although her book-writing days were over, from 1925 to 1943 she designed Christmas cards for Invalid Children's Aid, her favorite charity.

Not wanting the Lakelands developed and spoiled, Beatrix continued to buy all of the farm land that became available. In 1930 she bought the Monk Coniston Estate, 4000 acres, that went from Little Langdale to Coniston. It contained Tarn Hows, now Lakeland's most popular piece of landscape. Meanwhile, the National Trust was asking Beatrix for aid to preserve the Lakeland farms and countryside. Beatrix conceived the idea of selling original sketches through Miss Mahoney's Boston Bookshop for Boys and Girls. She sent a packet of fifty signed drawings to be sold, with the proceeds going to help the National Trust. Her concern for the future led her to work with the Trust's founder, her old friend Canon Hardwicke Rawnsley, who had given her encouragement to publish *Peter Rabbit*; and his encouragement was amply repaid when she set out to acquire land to present to the Trust for preservation.

When she died on 22 December, 1943, Beatrix Potter willed several farms, a number of cottages, 4000 acres of land, and her flocks of Herdwick sheep to be managed by the National Trust. Hill Top farm is exactly as Beatrix left it, and as you enter her 17th century farmhouse you take the exact route Tom Kitten took in his story, the *Roly-Poly Pudding*.

Hill Top

Many of the enchanting illustrations for Beatrix Potter's little tales were inspired by Hill Top, a charming 17th century house in Lakeland, where Beatrix Potter wrote many of her famous children's stories. Hill Top remains as she left it at her death, and in each room something can be found that appears in one of her books. The cottage garden contains the same mix of flowers, herbs, fruit, and vegetables that were originally grown by Beatrix Potter. Hill Top is a great example of a traditional English cottage and garden. There is a good variety of old fashioned flowers, such as honeysuckle, foxgloves, sweet cicely, lupines, peonies, lavender, and philadelphus. The ethereal rose grows around the front door.

Fruit has always played an important role in an English garden; strawberries, raspberries, currants, gooseberries, and rhubarb are still grown at Hill Top farm today.

Beatrix Potter bought Hill Top in 1905, with the royalties from her first few books, which she wrote at her parent's home in London but were inspired by her annual holiday visits to the Lake District. She visited Hill Top as often as she could, but never for more than a few days at a time; living with her parents in London until she married in 1913. During her visits, Beatrix Potter would sketch the house, garden, countryside, and animals — all inspirations for future books— and return to London to write.

English Sign Post in Sawrey near Hill Top farm.

A National Trust Sign Post for Hill Top Farm.

A view of Beatrix Potter's Hill Top farm. Currently operated by The National Trust.

Beatrix wrote and illustrated many of her famous children's stories in this little 17th century stone house. Characters such as Tom Kitten, Samuel Whiskers, and Jemima Puddle-duck were all created here, and the books contain many pictures influenced by the house and garden. Although she did not live at Hill Top full time, she filled the cottage with furniture and china and tended to the gardens.

When she died in 1943, she willed Hill Top to the National Trust, with the provision that it be kept exactly as she left it, complete with her furniture and china. In 1946 the National Trust opened Hill Top to the public. Over three million pairs of feet have walked through the five small rooms that are now available for public viewing. Over 70,000 visitors visit Hill Top each year. Today, some of her collections and original art works are displayed at the farm. It is open to the public during the summer months and is a must-see for all who love both Beatrix Potter and the Lakeland countryside, as well as environmentalists and the conservation-minded. For further information and prior to visiting, contact: hilltop@ntrust.org.uk

A close-up of Beatrix Potter's Hill Top farm. Hill Top is exactly as Beatrix Potter left it. Currently it is open to tourists.

Castle Cottage located on Castle Farm. During the negotiations for purchasing this property, Beatrix Potter met her future husband, William Heelis. After renovating Castle Cottage, the married couple resided here.

View of the Lake District countryside. Notice the Herdwick sheep, a tough native sheep that Beatrix Potter devoted herself to breeding. In 1930 Beatrix Potter became the first woman to become president of the Herdwick Sheep Breeders Association.

Beatrix Potter Books

While in London, Beatrix Potter made greeting cards of her many original illustrations. In 1890 she sent six designs for Christmas cards to the German firm of Hildesheimer & Faulkner, a greeting card publishing company. *The Happy Pair* (with verses by Frederick E. Weatherly) and other booklets were also published by Hildesheimer & Faulkner, featuring Beatrix Potter's illustrations made in 1890.

After Beatrix Potter's initial search for a commercial publishing company in 1901, and with Frederick Warne and Company publishing *The Tale of Peter Rabbit* in 1902, Frederick Warne and Company have owned the rights, copyrights, and trademarks in the Beatrix Potter character names and illustrations ever since. Beatrix Potter's original Peter Rabbit series include:

The Tale of Peter Rabbit
The Tale of Squirrel Nutkin
The Tailor of Gloucester
The Tale of Benjamin Bunny
The Tale of Two Bad Mice
The Tale of Mrs. Tiggy-Winkle
The Tale of The Pie and the Patty-Pan
The Tale of Mr. Jeremy Fisher
The Story of a Fierce Bad Rabbit
The Story of Miss Moppet
The Tale of Tom Kitten
The Tale of Jemima Puddle-Duck
The Tale of Samuel Whiskers or The Roly-Poly Pudding
The Tale of the Flopsy Bunnies

Ginger and Pickles
The Tale of Mrs. Tittlemouse
The Tale of Timmy Tiptoes
The Tale of Mr. Tod
The Tale of Pigling Bland
Appley Dapply's Nursery Rhymes
The Tale of Johnny Town-Mouse
Cecily Parsley's Nursery Rhymes
The Tale of Little Pig Robinson

NOTE: *Beatrix Potter The Complete Tales,* published by Frederick Warne, includes all 23 original stories in the Peter Rabbit series.

From 1923 to 1943 Beatrix Potter designed Christmas cards for Invalid Children's Aid, her favorite charity. She also wrote the following books, but they were not in the "Original Peter Rabbit Series":

Peter Rabbit's Almanac for 1929
The Fairy Caravan, 1929, published by David McKay Company, Philadelphia
The Fairy Caravan, 1952, published by Frederick Warne, London
Sister Anne, 1932, illustrated by Katherine Sturges, published by David McKay Company

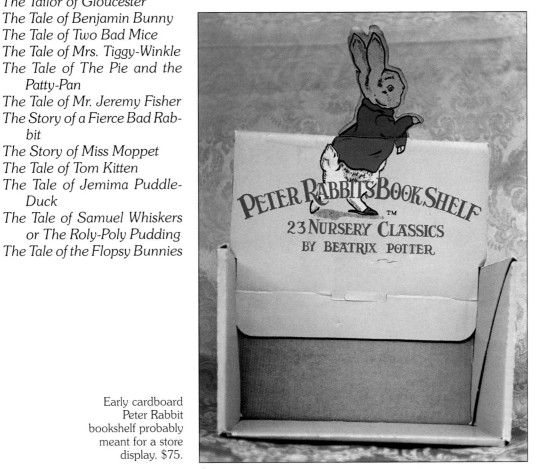

Early cardboard Peter Rabbit bookshelf probably meant for a store display. $75.

Sample of Beatrix Potter's *The Tale of Peter Rabbit* in Polish. $10.

Sample of Beatrix Potter's *The Tale of Peter Rabbit* in Latin and French. $10.

Sample of Beatrix Potter's *The Tale of Peter Rabbit* in Japanese and Portuguese. $10.

Sample of Beatrix Potter's *The Tale of Peter Rabbit* in Italian and Spanish. Book $10.

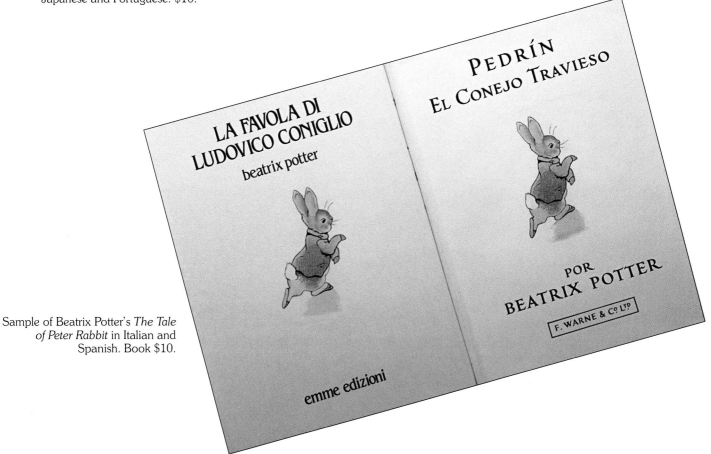

Beatrix Potter wrote several stories which were not published in her lifetime:

The Sly Old Cat, which she wrote in 1906, was published in 1971 by Frederick Warne

The Fox and the Stork, which she wrote in 1919 under the title *The Tale of Jenny Crow*

Wag-by-Wall, illustrated by J.J. Lankes, published in 1944 by The Horn Book, Inc., and again in 1987 by Frederick Warne, London. The 1987 publication was illustrated by Pauline Baynes

The Tale of the Faithful Dove was published in 1955 and in 1970 by Frederick Warne, illustrated by Marie Angel

The Tale of Tuppenny was published in 1973 by Frederick Warne, illustrated by Marie Angel

Country Tales was published in 1987 by Frederick Warne and illustrated by Pauline Baynes

During her lifetime, Beatrix Potter also made two picture sequences. The sequence of six paintings named "Three Little Mice" were six illustrations she drew in the 1890s to be used on greeting cards and as booklet illustrations. "The Rabbits' Christmas Party," a sequence of six paintings, was drawn in the 1890s.

The following synopsis is of the original Beatrix Potter Peter Rabbit series of books.

Sample of Beatrix Potter's *The Tale of Peter Rabbit* in Scottish and Chinese. $10.

Sample of Beatrix Potter's *The Tale of Peter Rabbit* in Welsh and German. $10.

THE TALE OF PETER RABBIT 1902

Beatrix Potter first introduced her naughty pet, Peter Rabbit, in a picture letter she wrote to Noel Moore, the five-year old son of her former governess, in 1893. Seven years later, Miss Potter borrowed the letter back and attempted to have it published into a little book, but received only rejections from companies she approached. With money received from her sale of greeting cards she had designed and sold, she decided to publish her book herself. That first printing was commissioned for 250 copies and Beatrix delighted in giving them to give to family and friends. Frederick Warne agreed to publish Peter Rabbit if Beatrix Potter would provide colored illustrations. Published in 1902, the Tale of Peter Rabbit, the story of a naughty rabbit that disobeys his mother's orders and runs into the garden of Mr. McGregor's, has never been out of print and is now available in over thirty-five foreign languages and in Braille.

The book and Squirrel Nutkin Beswick figurine with the gold oval mark from *The Tale of Squirrel Nutkin*. Figurine $225. Book $7.

The book and Peter Rabbit Beswick figurine with the gold oval mark from *The Tale of Peter Rabbit*. Figurine $175. Book $7.

THE TAILOR OF GLOUCESTER 1904

This engaging story occurs on Christmas Eve, the evening that folk lore suggests is the night animals talk. The town's tailor, suddenly ill and with no more cherry-colored thread (twist), is unable to finish the waistcoat for the pending Mayor's wedding. Simpkin, the Tailor's cat, is quite perturbed at his owner for releasing his food supply of mice. He is annoyed with the Tailor and hides the old man's much needed cherry-colored twist. The mice are very grateful that the Tailor has set them free and work feverishly into the evening to complete the Mayor's embroidered satin waistcoat. On Christmas morning, the Mayor of Gloucester was thrilled at the beautiful coat; soon word went out about the Tailor's talents and he became quite a wealthy gentleman. This delightful tale was Beatrix Potter's favorite among all the little books she had written and was dedicated to Freda Moore, another daughter of her former governess.

THE TALE OF SQUIRREL NUTKIN 1903

Squirrel Nutkin, another tale about a naughty animal by Beatrix Potter, also first appeared in a letter. This time the letter describing Squirrel Nutkin, a red squirrel that travels with other squirrels on a raft to an island to scoop up nuts, was written to Norah Moore, the eight-year old sister of Noel. While the other squirrels are busy collecting nuts, Squirrel Nutkin spends his time taunting and teasing Old Mr. Brown, the resident owl. In the end, Squirrel Nutkin must forever live with the consequences of his foolish behavior.

The book and The Tailor Beswick figurine with the gold oval mark from *The Tailor of Gloucester*. Figurine $145. Book $7.

THE TALE OF BENJAMIN BUNNY 1904

Benjamin Bunny, a beloved pet of Beatrix Potter, became the subject of his own tale in this sequel to *The Tale of Peter Rabbit*. Benjamin, Peter's bold cousin, persuades timid Peter that they both must return to Mr. McGregor's garden and retrieve Peter's lost blue jacket and shoes. They encounter many adventures in Mr. McGregor's garden, including being imprisoned under a basket filled with onions. They were held there by a large cat sitting on top until rescued by Benjamin's disgruntled father, old Mr. Bunny. This favorite tale of so many Beatrix Potter enthusiasts was dedicated for the children of Sawrey from old Mr. Bunny.

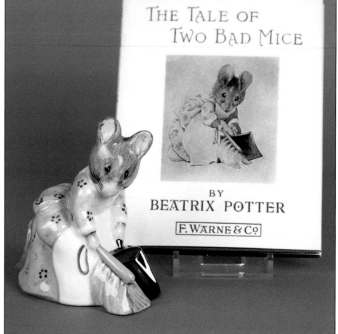

The book and Hunca Munca Sweeping new Beswick figurine with gold accents from *The Tale of Two Bad Mice*. Figurine $55. Book $7

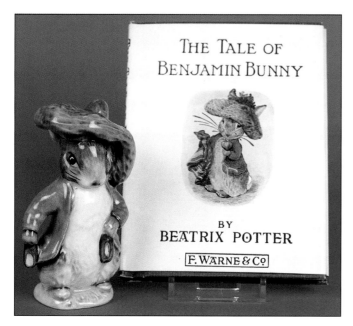

The book and Benjamin Bunny Beswick figurine (shoes and ears in) from *The Tale of Benjamin Bunny*. Figurine $80. Book $7.

THE TALE OF MRS. TIGGY-WINKLE 1905

Another beloved pet of Beatrix Potter's was the role model for this story of a washerwoman from Little-town. Mrs. Tiggy-winkle washes and irons Peter Rabbit's blue jacket and all of the clothing worn by her animal neighbors. Lucie, a little girl who lives nearby, visits Mrs. Tiggy-winkle to inquire about her missing pocket handkerchief and is quite surprised to discover that the washerwoman is really a hedgehog.

The book and Mrs. Tiggy-winkle Beswick figurine from *The Tale of Mrs. Tiggy-Winkle*. Figurine $100. Book $7.

THE TALE OF TWO BAD MICE 1904

This charming story involves Tom Thumb and his wife, Hunca Munca, two mice that discover to their delight a doll's house, complete with food on the table, and a fire in the fireplace. The two of them become so upset when they discover the food was made of plaster and the fireplace was crinkled red paper that they began to smash and break as much as possible. They decided that some part of the doll's house could be used in their own house and began carrying home items that fit into their own mouse-hole. In time, Tom Thumb felt badly about their actions and paid for everything they broke, and on Christmas Eve he left a crooked six-pence in the doll's stocking. Every morning since then, Hunca Munca quietly visits the doll's house to clean it.

THE TALE OF THE PIE AND THE PATTY-PAN 1905

This comical tale, set in the real village of Sawrey, located in Beatrix Potter's beloved Lake District in England brings together Duchess, a Pomeranian dog, and Ribby, a pussy-cat that are planning dinner together. Confusion and mistakes over food that was thought eaten makes this a very likeable tale. It is the one Beatrix Potter liked second to *The Tailor of Gloucester*. Beatrix dedicated this book to yet again another Moore child, Joan, to be read to Baby, Beatrix's goddaughter.

The book and Duchess with Pie Beswick figurine from *The Tale of The Pie and The Patty-Pan*. Figurine $500. Book $7.

THE TALE OF MR. JEREMY FISHER 1906

Mr. Jeremy Fisher first appeared in 1893 as a picture letter to Eric Moore, Noel's younger brother. Years later Beatrix found pleasure spending long hours sketching lovely, peaceful scenes in the Lake District. Mr. Jeremy Fisher is a frog that experiences a harrowing adventure as he attempts to catch minnows for his friends that he invites to dinner. This delightful book is filled with her beautiful illustrations of ponds, plants and the various forms of wildlife that live there.

The book and Mr. Jeremy Fisher Beswick figurine (spotted legs) from *The Tale of Mr. Jeremy Fisher*. Figurine $135. Book $7.

THE STORY OF A FIERCE BAD RABBIT 1906

The Story of a Fierce Bad Rabbit was written for very young children and the storyline is very simple describing how a naughty bad rabbit takes a carrot from a good little rabbit and the consequences that follow. This book was first released in panorama style, unfolding in a long strip, much like a wallet. It was a very unpopular style as it damaged easily. By 1916, this issue was reprinted in book form.

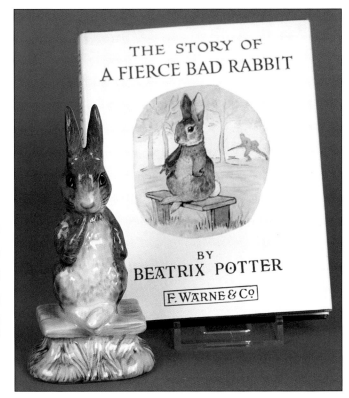

The book and Fierce Bad Rabbit Beswick figurine (feet out) from *The Story of a Fierce Bad Rabbit*. Figurine $175. Book $7.

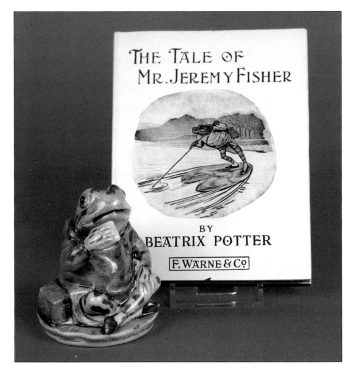

THE STORY OF MISS MOPPET 1906

Miss Moppet's story was also written for young readers and published in the panorama style like *The Story of a Fierce Bad Rabbit*. Moppet is Tom Kitten's sister, and this simple tale describes how Moppet first catches and then loses a little mouse. This book was reprinted in book form in 1916 to follow the same format of the publications already known as the series of Peter Rabbit books.

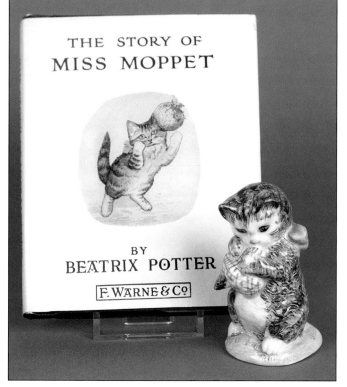

The book and Miss Moppet Beswick figurine (striped) from *The Story of Miss Moppet*. Figurine $80. Book $7.

THE TALE OF TOM KITTEN 1907

This is a favorite story for many Beatrix Potter enthusiasts because the author had been living happily in the Lake District village of Sawrey for over a year and the majority of the illustrations in this book are of inside her Hill Top farm and of her cottage garden.

Readers are able to visit the house and farm through the lives of Tabitha Twitchit and her three mischievous kittens who she has dressed properly to await the visit of friends invited for tea. The kittens, especially Tom, are unable to keep their clothing clean as they play and tumble outside and end up losing them completely to the puddle-ducks, who wore them into a pond.

The book and Tom Kitten Beswick figurine from *The Tale of Tom Kitten*. Figurine $140. Book $7.

THE TALE OF JEMIMA PUDDLE-DUCK 1908

Once again, Beatrix's lovely Hill Top farm is the background for this tale of a puddle-duck named Jemima that is determined to lay her eggs and keep them from the farmer's wife. While perusing the farm trying to find a safe location to lay her eggs, Jemima Puddle-duck meets a sandy-whiskered gentleman who volunteers to help in her search; but he is really a sly fox, with duck for dinner on his mind, and locks poor Jemima in a shed. With the help of Kep, the collie, Jemima is rescued but unfortunately loses her eggs to Kep's hungry puppies. Jemima Puddle-duck and Kep were just two of the many real-life pets and residences that lived at Hill Top. The book is dedicated to the children of John Cannon, the manager of Hill Top Farm.

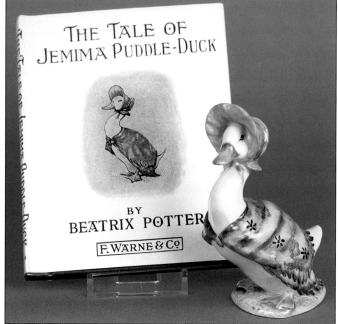

The book and Jemima Puddle-duck Beswick figurine from *The Tale of Jemima Puddle-Duck*. Figurine $80. Book $7.

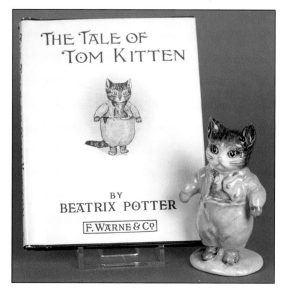

THE TALE OF SAMUEL WHISKERS or The Roly-Poly Pudding 1908

The inspiration for this tale was created when Beatrix was walking around Hill Top farm. She noticed many areas that would make good hiding places and homes for the large rodent population. This continuation of *The Tale of Tom Kitten* is a more suspenseful tale involving Tom and his family as they discover that a rat couple, with the intention of baking poor Tom into a roly-poly pudding, has abducted him. Tom is eventually saved but lives forever with a great fear of rats. The original title, in a larger format, *The Roly-Poly Pudding* was changed to *The Tale of Samuel Whiskers* in 1926; the same year it was reduced to the standard size of the other little books in the Peter Rabbit series. It was dedicated in remembrance to Beatrix's pet rat, Sammy, who was a very accomplished thief.

The book and Samuel Whiskers Beswick figurine from *The Tale of Samuel Whiskers or The Roly-Poly Pudding.* Figurine $115. Book $7.

THE TALE OF THE FLOPSY BUNNIES 1909

The Tale of the Flopsy Bunnies is another sequel involving the lives of Peter Rabbit and his cousin Benjamin Bunny. Both bunnies have grown up and Benjamin has married his cousin Flopsy and is raising a large family. Once again Mr. McGregor has caused another problem for the rabbits living nearby by capturing Benjamin's sleeping children, who along with their father, had eaten too many lettuces and drifted off to sleep. Thanks to Mrs. Tittlemouse, the bunnies were saved after she nibbled a hole in Mr. McGregor's sack to free them. Mrs. McGregor was not pleased when her husband returned home with a sack of rotten vegetables instead of the little bunnies he bragged about, but Mrs. Tittlemouse was very pleased with the Christmas present of rabbit-wool she received from Benjamin's grateful family.

The book and Mrs. Flopsy Beswick figurine from *The Tale of The Flopsy Bunnies.* Figurine $70. Book $7.

GINGER AND PICKLES 1909

The village of Sawrey was once again prominent in this fun story describing the business lives of shopkeepers, a yellow tom-cat called Ginger and his business partner—a terrier named Pickles, and the customers who frequent their little store. Characters from earlier Beatrix Potter books frequent the shop and continue to pay for their goods on credit, leaving no money in the till (cash register). With no money, Pickles cannot even afford his dog license. In time the little shop is closed, sending all the customers to Tabitha Twitchit's shop, were she shrewdly raised the prices on her goods. The town residences are very pleased when Sally Henny Penny opens her own store and keeps it supplied with goods that include bargains and something for everybody.

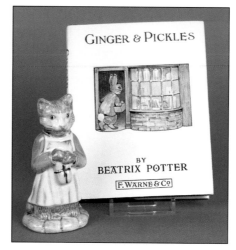

The book and Ginger Beswick figurine from *Ginger and Pickles*. Figurine $675. Book $7.

THE TALE OF MRS. TITTLEMOUSE 1910

Mrs. Tittlemouse, a wood-mouse, was a very clean little mouse who lived under a hedge. Uninvited creatures who lived nearby were always visiting bringing dirt, cobwebs, and muddy footprints with them. One day Mr. Jackson, a very untidy toad, makes an unexpected visit and when he departs Mrs. Tittlemouse's house is in such disarray that she wonders if it will ever be tidy again. After days of cleaning, Mrs. Tittlemouse, with the help of twigs, makes her door too small for large intruders like Mr. Jackson to enter.

She was so pleased with her clean house that she invited five mice friends for a party. Being a kind little mouse, she passed Mr. Jackson acorn-cupfuls of honeydew through an open window so he would not be offended.

THE TALE OF TIMMY TIPTOES 1911

Beatrix Potter had many American admirers and wrote and illustrated this story especially for them. The main characters; grey squirrels, chipmunks and even a black bear, were common animals in the United States, but not in England at the time. Timmy Tiptoes and his wife Goody set off to gather nuts in an area already occupied by many other squirrels with the same intentions. The other squirrels were busy burying their finds while Timmy and Goody stored their nuts in bags and placed them in hollow stumps near their home. When the stumps were filled to capacity, the Tiptoes emptied the bags down a woodpecker hole in a tree. The other squirrels accused Timmy of taking their nuts and forced him down a little hole in the ground. While trapped in the hole, Timmy eats too many nuts, gains weight and cannot fit out of the hole. While there, he meets a naughty chipmunk, Chippy Hackee who stays with Timmy instead of going home to his wife. In time, Timmy slims down and returns home. Chippy Hackee continues to live alone for another week until a bear arrives and frightens Chippy so much that he runs home.

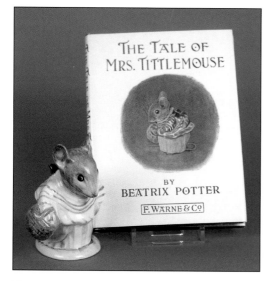

The book and Mrs. Tittlemouse Beswick figurine from *The Tale of Mrs. Tittlemouse*. Figurine $150. Book $7.

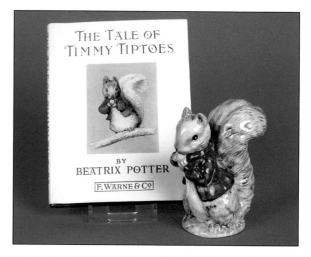

The book and Timmy Tiptoes Beswick figurine from *The Tale of Timmy Tiptoes*. Figurine $125. Book $7.

THE TALE OF MR. TOD 1912

Beatrix Potter thought it was time to introduce characters that were not nice and polite so she wrote about two very unlikable characters, Mr. Tod, a fox, and Tommy Brock, a badger. In this suspenseful tale, Tommy Brock has stolen Benjamin Bunny's children, which were being watched over by their aging grandfather, Old Mr. Bouncer. Tired from carrying the sack filled with seven bunnies, Tommy Brock stops to rest in a cave-like dwelling that is really a home belonging to Mr. Tod. Soon, the disagreeable fox returns to his home and discovers the sleeping intruder, Tommy Brock, and the entire home becomes a shamble as the two become involved in a ferrous battle. While the fighting continued outside, Benjamin Bunny and his cousin Peter Rabbit run into the severely damaged kitchen and rescue the little bunnies that are stored in the oven and soon they are returned safely to their own home.

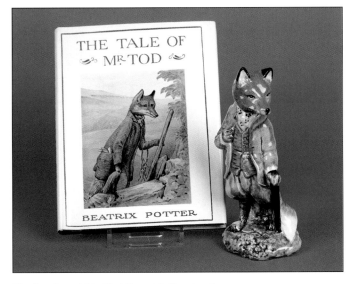

The book and Mr. Tod Beswick figurine from *The Tale of Mr. Tod*. Figurine $275. Book $7.

THE TALE OF PIGLING BLAND 1913

Pigling Bland is a pig that lives in the country with his seven brothers and sisters. Because the young pigs have such big appetites, Aunt Pettitoes decides all but Spot, the good little pig, must move on to new lives. She has acquired the correct licenses for Pigling Bland and his brother, Alexander, to go to market in Lancashire. Alexander soon loses his license forcing Pigling Bland to continue on his journey alone. Having never left home before, he incurs many adventures including a policeman, an ill-tempered farmer and a sweet black Berkshire pig named Pig-Wig. Pigling Bland really does not want to go to market but dreams of tending his own garden of potatoes. Both pigs seized the opportunity to escape and were last seen running hand-in-hand over the hills and far away.

APPLEY DAPPLY NURSERY RHYMES 1917

Although this book was published in 1917, it is compiled of many years of illustrations Beatrix created as early as 1893. It is a book with pages filled with Beatrix's endearing illustrations of mice, rabbits, a hedgehog, a mole, a pig, and an amiable guinea-pig, accompanied with her own nursery rhymes.

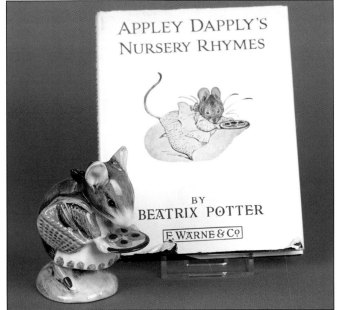

The book and Appley Dapply Beswick figurine (bottle in) from *Appley Dapply's Nursery Rhymes*. Figurine $70. Book $7.

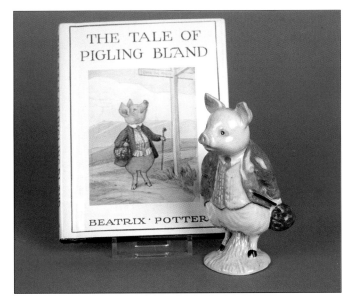

The book and Pigling Bland Beswick figurine (maroon jacket) from *The Tale of Pigling Bland*. Figurine $275. Book $7.

THE TALE OF JOHNNY TOWN-MOUSE 1918

This delightful story of two mice from distinctly different backgrounds is really derived from an Aesop Fable. Beatrix included scenes from her surroundings for both Johnny Town-mouse, a gentleman mouse that lives in the town and Timmy Willie, a country mouse that lives on a farm. Timmy accidentally falls asleep in a basket that is headed for the town residence of Johnny Town-mouse. His visit with Johnny and his dinner guests made him very nervous and he longed to return home. In time he did return home and hoped that his new friend from town would visit. In the spring, Johnny Town-mouse did call on Timmy Willie but did not like the quiet country lifestyle and returned happily to his own noisy home in town.

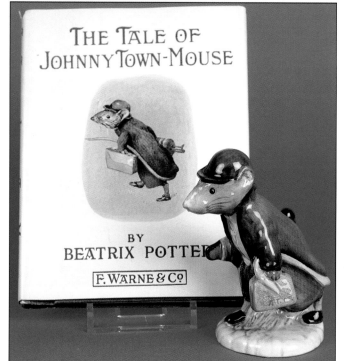

The book and Johnny Town-Mouse Beswick figurine from *The Tale of Johnny Town-Mouse*. Figurine $350. Book $7.

CECILY PARSLEY'S NURSERY RHYMES 1922

At this stage of her life, Beatrix's eyesight was failing and she was busy being a wife and farmer and had little time to write and illustrate stories. Like her previous book of nursery rhymes, this book too was a combination of illustrations and little verses written over a period of time. "The Guinea-Pigs' Garden" verses were illustrated decades before in 1893. This is a very endearing book of beautifully illustrated mice, rabbits, pigs, geese and more guinea pigs.

The book and Cecily Parsley Beswick figurine from *Cecily Parsley's Nursery Rhymes*. Figurine $125. Book $7.

THE TALE OF LITTLE PIG ROBINSON 1930

The last of the original Peter Rabbit books, this lengthy tale was created in her mind many years earlier in 1883, while Beatrix was vacationing by the coast in southern England. Little Pig Robinson is sent shopping by his aunts Dorcas and Porcas, which entails a long walk, but his adventure really begins when he is enticed to board a ship that soon leaves port with him on board. He is terrified when he discovers he is intended to be the Captain's special birthday dinner. Thankfully Susan, the ship's cat, saves him and he becomes a resident of an island in the South Seas.

Two editions were published simultaneously in 1930: one by Frederick Warne, Beatrix Potter's publisher in London, and another, in a larger format edition, that was published by David McKay Co., Philadelphia, Pennsylvania. The McKay edition contained several more black and white illustrations than the Warne edition.

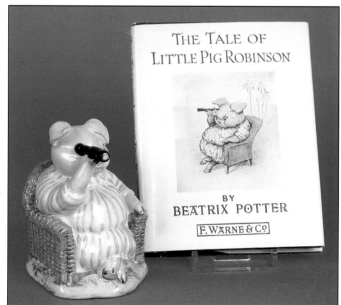

The book and Little Pig Robinson Spying Beswick figurine from *The Tale of Little Pig Robinson*. Figurine $225. Book $7.

Sought-after Beatrix Potter Collectibles

Beatrix Potter and Hill Top Collectibles

Collecting figurines and pieces with Beatrix Potter on them are very unique, rare and thus valuable and extremely sought after by collectors. In 1984 -Wedgwood produced, exclusively for the National Trust, an exquisite, limited to 1,000, Commemorative Beatrix Potter Plate. The 10" bone china plate features an illustration of Beatrix Potter, hat in hand, surrounded by sheep, looking down on the village of Sawrey. Individual illustrations of her characters grace the border. Antique items with Beatrix Potter herself on them are extremely rare and valuable.

Beatrix Potter's beloved Hill Top is currently an operational farm and historical tourist attraction. There are few collectible items featuring Hill Top but in 1993 Border Fine Arts produced a limited edition of 2,500 figurines of Hill Top. Today, if you can find this figurine on the secondary market, it would have a value of several hundred dollars.

1987 Royal Albert Beatrix Potter Cup. Issued in 1987 for The National Trust. $100.

Rare Border Fine Arts Tableau of Beatrix Potter and friends. $1000 up.

1987 Beatrix Potter Doll with Rabbit created by Ann Parker. $500.

1993 Border Fine Arts Limited Edition of 2,500 Hill Top. (Back) $350.

1993 Rockingham Pottery Limited Edition of 750. Beatrix Potter Figurine with Dog. $300.

1993 Border Fine Arts Limited Edition of 2,500 Hill Top. (Front) $350.

Grimwades Pottery

Formerly Grimwade Bros., established 1886
The Beatrix Potter Collection, 1900-1970s

Around 1908 Beatrix Potter began modeling her characters and self described them as "life like" and "comical". Smitten by Beatrix's characters, friend Katherine Smallfield, a director at the Royal Doulton, Lambeth Studio, England, recommended that she contact Joseph Mott the art director to determine if Royal Doulton would like to produce her beautiful tiny clay figures. Mr. Mott was excited to do so, but the project was muddled by a contract Royal Doulton had with a German firm who was contracted to make a range of nursery ware. Beatrix was very disappointed with the first Doulton characters and described them as "ugly" and urged her publishing company to get rid of the contracts so she could offer her characters to other firms.

It wasn't until 1917, when Beatrix received another unacceptable model of Jemima Puddle-duck produced by Elsie Grimwade (the daughter of Leonard Grimwade, a pottery manufacturer in Stoke-on-Trent, England), that she began making her own models once again. In 1918, Beatrix Potter corresponded with the Grimwades Company about the production of her molded clay figurines. She sent them to Grimwades but unfortunately most of them were broken during the shipping process. Beatrix waited through World War I and the delay in the production of china for her pieces of pottery. Finally in 1922 Grimwades began manufacturing her pieces of nursery ware, but we find no further documentation of the production of her figurines. Beatrix acted as a consultant for the illustrations on these nursery ware pieces and they were a huge success during that period. Illustrations and subjects recorded on the nursery ware were from the Tale of Peter Rabbit, The Tale of Tom Kitten, The Tale of Squirrel Nutkin, and The Tale of Jemima Puddle-Duck. Today, Grimwades have become very valuable and desired by Beatrix Potter collectors.

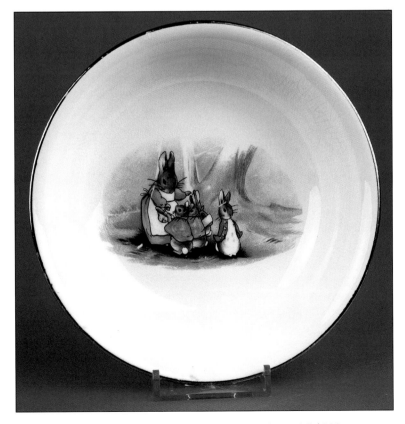

Rare Grimwade 6" Oatmeal Bowl "Mrs. Rabbit and Family" $300.

Collecting Peter Rabbit and His Friends

Beswick, Royal Doulton, Royal Albert: The Beatrix Potter Collection 1947-2002

In 1935 Beatrix Potter was approached by Walt Disney to get authorization to produce her many characters. Insulted, she would never allow her beloved Peter Rabbit to have characteristics like that famous mouse, she denied Disney's request. Walt Disney had never met a women like Beatrix Potter and when he was denied license, she made history by being the first ever to not contract her characters to be mass produced and marketed by the Walt Disney Corporation.

It was not until five years after Beatrix Potter's death that the first Beatrix Potter porcelain figurines were produced. It was Mrs. Lucy Beswick, the wife of the Chairman of the Beswick Company, who visited Hill Top and suggested that Jemima Puddle-duck might be an interesting character to mold. Their head modeler, Arthur Gredington began by borrowing the "Little Books" that belonged to the Beswick's daughter. In June 1947 Jemima Puddle-duck was ready to be inspected by Mr. Ewart Beswick. A few months after his approval, Frederick Warne and Company, gave the John Beswick Factory of Longton, Stoke-on-Trent, England the rights and licenses to produce Beatrix Potter's characters.

Beswick Tableau 3672, Mrs. Rabbit and the Four Bunnies, from *The Tale of Peter Rabbit*, 4 ½" length, Limited Edition Issued in 1997. $650.

MRS. RABBIT AND THE FOUR BUNNIES

The first ten characters; Jemima Puddle-duck, Peter Rabbit, Tom Kitten, Timmy Tiptoes, Squirrel Nutkin, Mrs. Tittlemouse, Little Pig Robinson, Benjamin Bunny, Samuel Whiskers, and Mrs. Tiggy-winkle started this collection as three to four and a half inch figurines and have grown to one hundred thirty-four figurines, twelve tableau, six character mugs, three plaques, three square embossed plaques or plates and seven resin studio sculptures. There are now figurines for characters from each of the twenty-three books. The Beswick porcelain figurines have been the most popular and well known figures. These figurines were first made with a backstamp that was "gold". The gold mark was changed to a second or brown mark by Royal Doulton about 1972. The brown backstamp was used until the third backstamp or John Beswick Signature Mark was introduced in 1988. Royal Albert and John Beswick are both part of the Royal Doulton family and since 1989 the Royal Albert backstamp with a crown has been used on the figure models as well as the nursery ware. These four distinctions can be used to date the figurines and some of the changes on the figures. The marks were only part of the changes. The detail and color of the painting of these figurines were much closer to the original illustration when the "gold marks" were used. The outer glaze had a lower gloss on the older "gold marked" figurines. Royal Doulton explains these as improvements in the glaze since the higher gloss coating will last longer with less crazing or cracking under the outer surface. It is the detail and deep, rich color, used on the figurines with the "gold" marks that make these figurines highly collectible in the secondary markets of figurines. Even though the marks have changed three times since the original "gold" mark was used the figurines have been made in the same building in England with the same process since 1948. For further information on the marks and variations in the figurines, see *John Beswick & Royal Albert Beatrix Potter Figures*, edited by Louise Irvine, and *The Charlton Standard Catalogue of Border Fine Arts and Storybook Figurines*, by Marilyn Sweet.

Following is a table of Beswick, Royal Doulton, and Royal Albert figurines arranged by the story, and with the model number, number of variations created, figurine name, date of copyright, and date it was retired.

Beswick Tableau 3867, Mrs. Tiggy-winkle and Lucie, from *The Tale of Mrs. Tiggy-Winkle*, 4" length, Limited Edition of 2,950 created. Issued in 1999. $300.

Original Beswick Peter Rabbit Commemorating the 100th birthday celebration with a facsimile of the original *The Tale of Peter Rabbit* book and original letter written by Beatrix Potter. Limited edition originally sold for $150. If found in perfect condition $320.

Very Rare Beswick Plaques Issued from 1967-1969 only. Left 2082, 6" high Jemima Puddle-duck Plaque, Center 2083, 6" Peter Rabbit Plaque, Right 2085, 6" high Tom Kitten Plaque. Value Depends on Condition $900-$1500 each.

Rare Beswicks. Left to Right: Simpkin, Ginger, Pickles from *The Tale of Ginger and Pickles*. Simpkin issued 1975-1983 $450. Ginger issued 1976-1982 $550. Pickles with gold mark $550 with brown mark $350-$400.

Back Side of the Rare Beswick Plaques of Jemima Puddle-duck, Peter Rabbit, and Tom Kitten. Note the marks and writing on bottoms.

Rare 1984 Beswick Sculpture of Mrs. Tiggy-winkle from *The Tale of Mrs. Tiggy-Winkle*. $350.

First Three Jugs Issued in 1987. Left Peter Rabbit from *The Tale of Peter Rabbit*. Right Mr. Jeremy Fisher from *The Tale of Mr. Jeremy Fisher* , Center Old Mr. Brown and Squirrel Nutkin from *The Tale of Squirrel Nutkin*. $200 each.

Rare 1985 Beswick Sculpture of the Flopsy Bunnies from *The Tale of The Flopsy Bunnies*. $350.

Second Jugs Issued in 1988. Mrs. Tiggy-winkle from *The Tale of Mrs. Tiggy-Winkle* , Tom Kitten from *The Tale of Tom Kitten* and Jemima Puddle-duck from *The Tale of Jemima Puddle-Duck*.. $200 each.

Royal Doulton Beswick Studio Sculpture. This is Timmy in the pea pod from *The Tale of Johnny Town-Mouse*. $250.

Edens: Mr. Jeremy Fisher, Jemima Puddle-duck and Peter Rabbit taking tea on 1986 Royal Albert Tea Set. Giant Eden's $200 each. Tea Set $500.

1986 Royal Albert Tea Set. Note Giant Eden of Mrs. Rabbit in the background. Tea Set $500. Giant Eden $200.

Giant Eden of Mr. Jeremy Fisher with 1986 Royal Albert Character Tea Cup. Giant Eden $200. Tea Cup $150.

Model No.	Variations	Name	© Date	Date Retired
		Figurines from The Tale of Peter Rabbit		
1098	4	Peter Rabbit	1948	2002
1200	2	Mrs. Rabbit	1951	2002
1274	0	Flopsy, Mopsy, Cottontail	1954	1997
2083	0	Peter Rabbit Plaque	1967	1969
2650	0	Peter Rabbit Plaque (Embossed Plate)	1979	1983
3157	0	Peter Rabbit in the Gooseberry Net	1989	1995
3006	0	Peter Rabbit Mug	1987	1992
3278	0	Mrs. Rabbit Cooking	1992	1999
3356	2	Peter Rabbit (Large Size) Special 100th Anniversary Mark (Second version limited edition)	1993	1997
3398	2	Mrs. Rabbit (Large Size) (Second version limited edition)	1994	1998
3506	0	Mr. McGregor	1995	2002
3533	0	Peter Ate a Radish	1995	1998
3646	0	Mrs. Rabbit and Peter	1997	2002
3888	0	Sweet Peter (Limited Edition)	1999	1999
3473	0	Peter in Bed	1995	2002
3672	0	Mrs. Rabbit and the Four Bunnies Tableau (Limited Edition)	1997	1997
3940	0	Peter in the watering can	1999	2002
3978	0	Mrs. Rabbit and Peter (Limited Edition)	1999	1999
4161	0	Flopsy, Mopsy and Cottontail Tableau (Limited Edition)	2002	2002
4217	0	Peter on His Book	2002	2002

Model No.	Variations	Name	© Date	Date Retired
		Figurines from The Tale of Squirrel Nutkin		
1102	2	Squirrel Nutkin	1948	2000
1796	0	Old Mr. Brown	1963	1999
2959	0	Old Mr. Brown Mug	1987	1992
3893		Squirrel Nutkin (Large Size, Limited Edition)	1999	1999
		Figurines from The Tailor of Gloucester		
1108	0	Tailor of Gloucester	1949	2002
1183	0	Lady Mouse	1950	2000
2508	0	Skimpkin	1975	1983
3200	0	Gentleman Mouse Made a Bow	1990	1996
3220	0	Lady Mouse Makes a Curtsy	1990	1997
3325	0	No More Twist	1992	1997
3449	2	Tailor of Gloucester (Large Size)(Second version larger)	1995	1997
		Figurines from The Tale of Benjamin Bunny:		
1105	5	Benjamin Bunny	1948	2002
1940	2	Old Mr. Benjamin Bunny	1965	2000
2509	0	Mr. Benjamin Bunny with Peter Rabbit	1975	1995
2543	0	Mrs. Rabbit with Bunnies	1976	1997
2560	0	Poorly Peter Rabbit	1976	1997
2803	2	Benjamin Bunny Sat on a Bank	1983	1997
3242	0	Peter and the Red Pocket Handkerchief	1991	1999
3317	0	Benjamin Ate a Lettuce Leaf	1992	1998
3403	2	Benjamin Bunny (Large Size) (Second version larger)	1994	1997
5190	0	Peter and the Red Pocket Handkerchief (Limited Edition)	1997	1997
3592	2	Peter with Red Handkerchief (Large Size)	1996	1998
3672	0	Hiding from the Cat Tableau (Limited Edition)	1998	1998
3930	0	Peter and Benjamin Picking Up Onions Tableau (Limited Edition)	2000	2000
		Figurines from The Tale of Two Bad Mice		
1198	0	Hunca Munca With Cradle	1951	2000
2584	2	Hunca Munca Sweeping	1977	2002
2989	0	Tom Thumb	1987	1997
3257	0	Christmas Stocking	1991	1994
3288	0	Hunca Munca Spills the Beads	1992	1996
3894	0	Hunca Munca (Large Size, Limited Edition)	1999	1999
4074	0	Hunca Munca	2001	2002
		Figurines from The Tale of Mrs. Tiggy-Winkle		
1107	4	Mrs. Tiggy-winkle	1948	2002
2877	0	Mrs. Tiggy-winkle Takes Tea	1985	2002
3102	0	Mrs. Tiggy-winkle Mug	1988	1992
3437	2	Mrs. Tiggy-winkle (Large Size) (Second version larger)	1996	1998
3789	0	Mrs. Tiggy-winkle Washing	1998	2000

Model No.	Variations	Name	© Date	Date Retired
3867	0	Mrs. Tiggy-winkle and Lucie Tableau (Limited Edition of 2,950)	1999	1999

Figurines from The Tale of Mr. Jeremy Fisher

Model No.	Variations	Name	© Date	Date Retired
1157	3	Mr. Jeremy Fisher	1950	2002
2424	0	Mr. Alderman Ptolemy	1973	1997
2425	0	Sir Isaac Newton	1972	1984
3090	0	Mr. Jeremy Fisher Digging	1988	1994
2960	0	Mr. Jeremy Fisher Mug	1987	1992
3372	2	Mr. Jeremy Fisher (Large size) (Second version larger)	1994	1998
3919	0	Mr. Jeremy Fisher Catches a Fish	1999	2002

Figurines from The Tale of Tom Kitten

Model No.	Variations	Name	© Date	Date Retired
1100	3	Tom Kitten	1948	1999
2085	0	Tom Kitten Plaque	1967	1969
2544	0	Tabitha Twitchit and Miss Moppet	1976	1993
2628	0	Mr. Drake Puddle-duck	1979	2000
2647	0	Mrs. Rebeccah Puddle-duck	1981	2000
3030	0	Tom Kitten with Butterfly	1987	1994
3197	0	Mittens and Moppet	1990	1994
3103	0	Tom Kitten Mug	1988	1992
3405	2	Tom Kitten (Large Size) (Second version larger)	1994	1997
3719	0	Tom Kitten in the Rockery	1998	2002
3792	0	Mittens, Tom Kitten and Moppet Tableau	1999	1999
4020	0	Tabitha Twitchit and Miss Moppet (Large Size) (Second version larger)	2000	2000

Figurines from The Tale of Jemima Puddle-Duck

Model No.	Variations	Name	© Date	Date Retired
1092	3	Jemima Puddle-duck	1948	2002
1277	2	Foxy Whiskered Gentleman	1954	2002
2594	0	Jemima Puddle-duck with Foxy Whiskered Gentlemen Plaque (Embossed Plate)	1977	1982
2823	0	Jemima Puddle-duck Made a Feather Nest	1983	1997
3193	0	Jemima Puddle-duck and Foxy Whiskered Gentleman	1990	1999
3219	0	Foxy Whiskered Gentleman Reading Country News	1990	1997
3088	0	Jemima Puddle-duck Mug	1987	1992
3373	2	Jemima Puddle-duck (Large Size) (Second version larger) 1994 Issued with special Beswick Commermorative Mark	1993	1998
3450	2	Foxy Whiskered Gentleman (Large Size) (Second version larger)	1995	1997
3786	0	Jemima Puddle-duck and Her Ducklings	1998	2002
4901	0	Kep and Jemima Tableau (Limited Edition of 2000)	2002	2002

Figurines from The Tale of Flopsy Bunnies

Model No.	Variations	Name	© Date	Date Retired
1942	0	Mrs. Flopsy Bunny	1965	1998
2668	0	Mrs. Thomasina Tittlemouse	1981	1989
3234	0	Benjamin Bunny Wakes Up	1991	1997
4155	0	Flopsy and Benjamin Bunny Tableau	2001	2002

Model No.	Variations	Name	© Date	Date Retired
4075	0	Peter Rabbit Digging	2001	2002

Figurines from The Tale of Mrs. Tittlemouse

Model No.	Variations	Name	© Date	Date Retired
1103	0	Mrs. Tittlemouse	1948	1993
2453	2	Mr. Jackson	1974	1997
2685	0	Mrs. Tittlemouse Plaque (Embossed Plate)	1982	1984
2966	0	Mother Lady Bird	1989	1996
2971	0	Babbitty Bumble	1989	1993
4015	0	Mrs. Tittlemouse	2000	2002

Figurines from The Tale of Timmy Tiptoes

Model No.	Variations	Name	© Date	Date Retired
1101	2	Timmy Tiptoes	1948	1997
1675	0	Goody Tiptoes	1961	1997
2627	0	Chippy Hackee	1979	1993
2957	0	Goody and Timmy Tiptoes	1986	1996

Figurines from The Tale of Mr. Tod

Model No.	Variations	Name	© Date	Date Retired
1348	4	Tommy Brock	1955	2002
2956	0	Old Mr. Bouncer	1986	1995
3091	0	Mr. Tod	1988	1993

Figurines from The Tale of Pigling Bland

Model No.	Variations	Name	© Date	Date Retired
1365	2	Pigling Bland	1955	1998
2276	0	Aunt Pettitoes	1970	1993
2381	0	Pig- wig	1972	1982
3252	0	Pigling eats his Porridge	1991	1994
3946	0	Yock-Yock in the tub	2000	2002

Figurines from The Tale of Johnny Town-Mouse

Model No.	Variations	Name	© Date	Date Retired
1109	0	Timmy Willie	1949	1993
1276	0	Johnny Town-mouse	1954	1993
2996	0	Timmy Willie Sleeping	1986	1996
3094	0	Johnny Town-mouse with Bag	1988	1994
3931	0	Johnny Town-mouse Eating Corn	2000	2002
3976	0	Timmy Willie Fetching Milk	2000	2002

Figurines from The Tale of Samuel Whiskers or The Roly-Poly Pudding

Model No.	Variations	Name	© Date	Date Retired
1106	0	Samuel Whiskers	1948	1995
1676	2	Mrs. Tabitha Twitchit	1961	1995
1851	0	Anna Maria	1963	1983
2284	0	Cousin Ribby	1970	1993
2965	0	John Joiner	1990	1997
4014	0	Farmer Potatoes	2000	2002
4169	0	My Dear Son Thomas Tableau (Limited Edition)	2001	2001

Figurines from The Tale of the Pie and the Patty Pan

Model No.	Variations	Name	© Date	Date Retired
1199	0	Ribby	1951	2000
1355	0	Duchess with Flowers	1955	1967

Model No.	Variations	Name	© Date	Date Retired
2601	0	Duchess with Pie	1979	1982
3280	0	Ribby and the Patty Pan	1992	1998
3983	0	Duchess and Ribby Tableau (Limited Edition)	2000	2000

Figurines from The Tale of Ginger and Pickles

2334	0	Pickles	1970	1982
2452	0	Sally Henny Penny	1974	1993
2559	0	Ginger	1976	1982
3251	0	Miss Dormouse	1991	1995
3790	0	Ginger and Pickles (Tableau) (Limited Edition)	1998	1998
4243	0	Mrs. Tiggy-winkle Buys Provisions	2002	2002

Figurines from The Tale of Little Pig Robinson

1104	2	Little Pig Robinson	1948	1999
2716	0	Susan	1983	1989
3031	0	Little Pig Robinson Spying	1987	1993

Figurines from The Story of a Fierce Bad Rabbit

2586	0	Fierce Bad Rabbit	1977	1997

Figurines from The Story of Miss Moppet

1275	2	Miss Moppet	1954	2002

Figurines from Appley Dapply's Nursery Rhymes

1545	0	Old Woman Who Lived in a Shoe	1959	1998
2061	0	Amiable Guinea Pig	1967	1983
2333	2	Appley Dapply	1971	2002
2585	0	Little Black Rabbit	1977	1997
2713	0	Diggory Diggory Delvet	1983	1989
2767	0	Old Mr. Pricklepin	1983	1989
2804	0	Old Woman who Lived in a Shoe, Knitting	1983	2002
2878	0	Mrs. "Cottontail" at Lunchtime	1985	1996
4031	0	Amiable Guinea-pig	2000	2002
4210	0	Two Gentlemen Rabbits (From End Papers)	2002	2002

Figurines from Cecily Parsley's Nursery Rhymes

1941	2	Cecily Parsley	1965	1993
3319	0	And This Pig Had None	1992	1998
4030	0	This Pig had a bit of Meat (Limited Edition)	2000	2000
4236	0	Head Gardener	2002	2002

Figurines from Peter Rabbit's Almanac for 1929

3591	0	Peter Rabbit with Postbag (Cover)	1996	2002
3597	0	Peter Rabbit with Daffodils (May)	1996	1999
3739	0	Peter Rabbit Gardening	1998	1999
4160	0	Peter and Benjamin Picking Apples Tableau (Limited Edition)	2002	2002

An antique pine cupboard full of Peter Rabbit and Mrs. Tiggy-winkle Wedgwood Nursery Ware.

Wedgwood—
The Beatrix Potter Collection 1949-2002

The Original Peter Rabbit Design Nursery Ware

The English company, Josiah Wedgwood & Sons, Ltd., has been licensed to produce nursery ware featuring Peter Rabbit since 1949. Their first design was for the export market and consisted of ten different items which included a breakfast plate, tea plate, oatmeal bowl, milk jug, cup and saucer, mug, two different sized cream jugs, and an egg cup Pattern No. CM6466 which is part of the back stamp.

In 1955 the backstamp changed to Pattern No. CM6522. Wedgwood factory records indicate that two pattern changes were entered in 1957 as follows: 'NM526, cream colored earthenware nursery set, Peter Rabbit lithograph, edge line in dark green and 'NM527, cream colored earthenware nursery ware, Peter Rabbit lithograph on-glaze, with no edge line. The motifs remained the same. This is a very beautiful series of dishes with vibrant illustrations in the middle of each item surrounded by green ivy and various other Beatrix Potter characters as depicted in the end papers of the Peter Rabbit books.

The Original Peter Rabbit design of the Peter Rabbit Wedgwood Nursery Ware, Tea Cup and Saucer. $150.

Peter Rabbit Wedgwood Plate 7" 1969-2001. $40.

A set of the Original Peter Rabbit design of the Peter Rabbit Wedgwood Nursery Ware. Individual pieces from $80-$100 each. Set $300.

Peter Rabbit Nursery Ware Quotations

In late 1969 Wedgwood retired their prior series and introduced an entirely new series of Peter Rabbit nursery ware entitled "Peter Rabbit Quotations." It was called this because each quotation came from the book *The Tale of Peter Rabbit* coinciding with the appropriate illustration. This extremely popular series of various dishes known as Queen's Ware was produced for over thirty years with production ceasing in 2001. Each dish was made of white earthenware and featured an original illustration from *The Tale of Peter Rabbit* with the story line from the book in bold black lettering. Over the years new dish styles were added and retired. A collector of the 'Peter Rabbit Quotations' range may own over 60 assorted pieces of this nursery ware ranging from everyday items such as various sized plates, bowls, egg coddles, egg cups, porringers, mugs, beakers, and lamp, to giftware items such as cachepots, chamber pots, various trinket boxes, soap dishes, plaques, tea pot stands, table bells, various styled banks and clocks, and even a child's ten piece tea set and adult sized tea set.

A few items were created for the British market, specifically the odd shaped paper weight and finger door plate. The light switch plate was created for the market in the United States. In honor of Prince William's impending birth in 1982, a plate and a mug were issued in England and Canada titled "Welcome to the New Baby of the Prince and Princess of Wales, With Love, Peter Rabbit."

In 1983 Wedgwood began producing a Benjamin Bunny mug with quotations from the illustrations in green sentences and a Jemima Puddle-duck mug with blue sentences.

Beginning in 1993 and continuing to 2001, Wedgwood began adding new and varied series of Peter Rabbit nursery and gift ware. First there was a set of six Peter Rabbit storybook wall plaques with illustrated scenes from *The Tale of Peter Rabbit* but with no quotations. Following that series was the Peter Rabbit Centennial (1893-1993) collection honoring Peter's 100th anniversary. This delightful set of six individual pieces featured Peter Rabbit illustrations with quotations and sentences produced from Beatrix Potter's handwriting. This collection was available for one year only.

As a note of interest there is a platter, bowl and large mug that features illustrations from *The Tale of The Flopsy Bunnies* that are marked "Peter Rabbit Wedgwood 1996." Their designs are faded and are poor quality and they were purchased from discount stores. The same is true for several Wedgwood dishes marked "The Peter Rabbit and Benjamin Bunny Collection." To add to the confusion with this series, there is one illustrated plate, three different illustrated mugs and three different illustrated bowls, all with different copyrighted years: 1996, 1998, and 1999.

Peter Rabbit Wedgwood Compotier 6" 1974-1999. $35.

Peter Rabbit Small and Large Egg Coddlers c. 1974-1983. $75 each.

Peter Rabbit Wedgwood Oatmeal Bowl, 6" 1969-2001. $35.

Prior to the mid-1990s, there was absolutely no way to differentiate or authenticate an older piece from a newer piece of Peter Rabbit Nursery Ware. Some pieces in the collection were produced for several consecutive years but due to the fact that a collector can not tell the age of a piece by its markings, a piece that was issued earlier is not more valuable than a newer piece. Of course, the condition of a piece of Peter Rabbit Nursery Ware is paramount and will affect the value.

Peter Rabbit Wedgwood Tea Set; each sold individually. Tea Cup and Saucer introduced in 1974, Tea Pot 1983, Cream Jug 1983, Sugar Box with Lid 1983. This set was retired in 1997. Complete Set $400 up.

Peter Rabbit Unique Wedgwood Snack Bowl 4" 1987-1988. $50.

Peter Rabbit Wedgwood Jug 0.5 pt 1974-1988 $75. Wedgwood Honey Pot with Lid 1976-1988 $100.

Peter Rabbit Wedgwood Bowl 8" 1989-1992. $100.

Rare and collectible Wedgwood Peter
Rabbit Chamber Pot, 1982-1985. $200.

Wedgwood Peter Rabbit Egg Box with Lid 4.25"
1982-1985. $150.

Highly collectible Peter Rabbit Wedgwood
Paper Weight, 1987-1988. $200.

Wedgwood Peter Rabbit
Heart Box with Lid
1982-1991. $250.

Wedgwood Peter Rabbit Round Box with Lid 1987-1991. $100.

Wedgwood Peter Rabbit Treasure
Chest with Lid, 1987-1991. $100.

Wedgwood Peter Rabbit Piggy Bank 1996-1999. $50.

Peter gave himself up for lost, and shed big tears; but his sobs were overheard by some friendly sparrows.

Wedgwood Peter Rabbit Hexagon Money Box 1974-1988. $75.

THE TALE OF PETER RABBIT
THE TALE OF MRS. TIGGY-WINKLE
THE TALE OF BENJAMIN BUNNY
THE TALE OF JEMIMA PUDDLE-DUCK
THE TALE OF PETER RABBIT

Wedgwood Peter Rabbit Unusual Bank Book Ends
1989-1990. Pair $350 up.

Wedgwood Peter Rabbit Cache Pot 1989-1992. $125.

Wedgwood Peter Rabbit Soap Dish 1982-1988. $125.

Wedgwood Peter Rabbit
Table Bell 1982-1988. $175.

Wedgwood Peter Rabbit Silver Tray (for coins) 1982-1988. $50.

Wedgwood Peter Rabbit Sandwich Tray 1985-1992. $100.

Once upon a time there were four little Rabbits, and their names were- Flopsy, Mopsy, Cotton tail, and Peter.

Wedgwood Peter Rabbit Pencil Tray 1985-1991. $100.

Wedgwood Peter Rabbit Children's Double Handled Mugs. Right Mug is the new revised mug, which came out in 1995 and was retired in 2000. $35 each.

Wedgwood Peter Rabbit original classic Mug 1969-2000. $40.

Wedgwood Peter Rabbit Jug 1.25 pt 1989-1992. $90.

Wedgwood Peter Rabbit revised Mug 1993-2001. $35.

Wedgwood Peter Rabbit Treat Basket 1996-1999. $100.

Wedgwood Peter Rabbit Beaker 1982-1991. $60.

Wedgwood Peter Rabbit Children's Tea Set 1979-2000. Set $150 up.

Wedgwood Peter Rabbit
Snack Bowl, 6" 1996. $50.

Wedgwood Peter Rabbit Centennial Set
1993. The script on this set is Beatrix
Potter's handwriting. The set is in honor
of Peter Rabbit's 100th birthday. $400 up.

Wedgwood Peter Rabbit Christening Dishes 1993-2000. Set $250 up.

Wedgwood Peter Rabbit Happy Birthday Dishes 1997-2000. Set $150.

Wedgwood Peter Rabbit Tea Time 1996-2000. Note the absence of quotations. Set $100.

Wedgwood Peter Rabbit Christmas Set 1996-2000. Set $200.

Wedgwood Peter Rabbit ABC Set 1997-2000. Set $90.

Wedgwood Peter Rabbit Centennial Set; Plate and Mug 2002. This set is in honor of the publication of the book *The Tale of Peter Rabbit* in 1902. Set $75.

Wedgwood Peter Rabbit Millennium 8" Plate and 8-ounce mug produced only in 2000. $100 for set.

The Tailor of Gloucester Wedgwood Centennial Set; Plate and Mug 2003. This set is in honor of the publication of the book *The Tailor of Gloucester* in 1903. Set $75.

Wedgwood Commemorative Plate for the birth of Prince William,
the future Prince of England. 1982-1983. Set $200.

Mrs. Tiggy-winkle Nursery Ware

In 1979, Mrs. Tiggy-winkle became a series of new Wedgwood Queen's Ware Nursery Ware. It featured original illustrations from Beatrix Potter's book, *The Tale of Mrs. Tiggy-Winkle*, and a story line quotation printed in brown. All of the individual pieces, including a separate child's ten piece tea set, were the same style of plates, mug, porringer, etc., that were available in the Peter Rabbit series. Only sixteen items were produced in the Mrs. Tiggy-winkle line and the complete series was retired in 1995.

Sample of Mrs. Tiggy-winkle Wedgwood
Nursery Ware. Set $300. A Giant Eden
of Mrs. Tiggy-winkle sitting in chair. $200.

Mrs. Tiggy-winkle Wedgwood adult set of 9", 8", and 7" Plates. $40 each.

Mrs. Tiggy-winkle Wedgwood Cup and Saucer. $45.

Mrs. Tiggy-winkle Wedgwood Children's
Nursery Ware Tea Set. $200.

Mrs. Tiggy-winkle Wedgwood Oval Money Box 1988-1991. $60.

Mrs. Tiggy-winkle on Wedgwood Annual Birthday Plate. The only year that a character other than Peter Rabbit was used on the annual plate. Rare and valuable. $200.

Mrs. Tiggy-winkle Wedgwood Egg Candy Box 1974, retired in 1985. $175.

Peter Rabbit and Benjamin Bunny Nursery Ware

As a note of interest there is a platter, bowl and large mug that features illustrations from *The Tale of Benjamin Bunny* that are marked "The Peter Rabbit and Benjamin Bunny Collection." Their designs are faded and are poor quality and they were purchased from discount stores. To add to the confusion with this series, there is one illustrated plate, three different illustrated mugs and three different illustrated bowls, all with different copyrighted years: 1996, 1998, and 1999. As a note of interest in 1997, Wedgwood used a tin to house a mug and oatmeal bowl from *The Tale of Benjamin Bunny*. There is no further information on this line available.

1997 Wedgwood Tin, unique as it is the only known tin used to contain collectible Wedgwood pieces. Housed a mug and oatmeal bowl. From *The Tale of Benjamin Bunny*. $40.

Wedgwood Oatmeal Bowl 6" "Little Benjamin Said…" 1996. From *The Tale of Benjamin Bunny*. $40.

Wedgwood Oatmeal Bowl 6" "Benjamin on the Contrary…" 1999. From *The Tale of Benjamin Bunny*. $40.

Wedgwood Oatmeal Bowl 6" "Peter - Said Little Benjamin…" 1998. From *The Tale of Benjamin Bunny*. $40.

Wedgwood Plate 1999. From *The Tale of Benjamin Bunny*. $35.

Set of Wedgwood Mugs. Far Left Mug "Benjamin tried on…" 1996. Middle Mug "Benjamin Nearly Tumbles…" 1998. Right Mug 1983. All from *The Tale of Benjamin Bunny*. $35 each.

In 1983 Benjamin Bunny (words in green) and Jemima Puddle-duck (words in blue) Wedgwood Mugs were issued. $50 each.

Wedgwood Annual Plate Collection

In 1981 Wedgwood introduced a brand new series of Peter Rabbit Queen's Ware in the form of an annual Christmas and birthday plate. The early annual Peter Rabbit Christmas plates are very similar to the birthday plates except the border of characters includes ribbons, bows, bells and presents with a red rim and the message reads "Peter Rabbit wishes you a very Merry Christmas." The annual birthday plate was issued as a companion to the annual Christmas plate. The first birthday plate titled: "Peter Rabbit wishes you a very Happy Birthday" featured a Peter Rabbit illustration, surrounded by the twelve Beatrix Potter characters, replicating the end papers in the Peter Rabbit books series, with a blue line around the rim.

1982 Christmas Plate "Mrs. Rabbit giving Peter Chamomile Tea" from *The Tale of Peter Rabbit*. $40.

1981 Christmas Plate "Peter Rabbit Under the Gate" from *The Tale of Peter Rabbit*. $40.

1983 Christmas Plate "Rabbits Under an Umbrella" from a 1894 painting first issued as a Christmas Card in 1925 for the Invalid Children's Aid Association. $40.

The illustrations on the 1984-1987 annual Christmas plates were from "The Rabbits' Christmas Party" a sequence of charming paintings Beatrix Potter painted in the early 1890s. 1984 Christmas Plate "The Guests Arrive." $40.

1986 Christmas Plate "Rabbits Baking Toffee Apples." $40.

1985 Christmas Plate "Dinner is Served." $40.

1987 Christmas Plate "Time to go Home." $40.

1989 Christmas Plate a repeat illustration featured on 1982 Christmas plate of "Mrs. Rabbit giving Peter chamomile tea" from *The Tale of Peter Rabbit*. $40.

1988 Christmas Plate "Mrs. Rabbit Buttoning Peter's Blue Coat." Note the border design change and the illustration returned to *The Tale of Peter Rabbit*. $40.

1990 Christmas Plate of "Peter eating radishes" from *The Tale of Peter Rabbit*. $40.

1991 Christmas Plate of "Mrs. Rabbit with her children" from *The Tale of Peter Rabbit*. $40.

1992 Christmas Plate of "Peter feeling ill" from *The Tale of Peter Rabbit*. $30.

1993 Christmas Plate of rabbit with letter and cauliflower from a 1935 greeting card illustration. $30.

New border design is introduced in 1994. The illustration possibly from an early 1890s Christmas card. 1994 Christmas Plate of "Four Rabbits in Snow." $30.

1996 Christmas Plate "The Gift" from the cover illustration of *Changing Pictures*, a booklet published by Ernest Nister in 1894. $30.

1995 Christmas Plate January illustration of rabbit shoveling snow from *Peter Rabbit's Almanac* of 1929. $30.

1997 Christmas Plate "The Visit" possibly a design intended for a Christmas card for Hildesheimer & Faulkner, a greeting card publisher. $30.

1998 Christmas Plate. One of six c. 1892, illustrations known as "The Rabbits' Christmas Party." $30.

1999 Christmas Plate. Sleigh Ride is an early c.1894 watercolor depicting "Bunnies in the Snow." $30.

Note a new, darker and bolder border design is featured on the 2000-2003 Christmas editions. 2000 Christmas Plate depicts an illustration of Peter Rabbit and Benjamin Bunny peering into the bedroom window of Tommy Brock's kitchen from *The Tale of Mr. Tod*. $30.

2001 Christmas Plate *Ginger and Pickles* from *The Tale of Ginger and Pickles*. $30.

2002 Christmas Plate "A Happy Pair" from a 1890 Beatrix Potter illustration that was included in a booklet called *A Happy Pair* for the Publisher Hildesheimer & Faulkner. $30.

Originally Wedgwood intended to feature a different character ever year, and in 1982 Mrs. Tiggy-winkle was featured on the 1982 birthday plate. But, in 1983 the decision was made to feature exclusively Peter Rabbit and the plate series continued to feature exclusively Peter Rabbit. Not every illustration is from *The Tale of Peter Rabbit*, but the quotation was always from *The Tale of Peter Rabbit*. Several illustrations have been from *The*

Peter Rabbit's Almanac of 1929 and various greeting cards. No Peter Rabbit birthday plates were issued in 1987 or 1988 because for those two years, Wedgwood decided to produce plates featuring Oakapple Wood character designs. Approximately every five years Wedgwood changed the border designs on both their Christmas and birthday annual plates.

1981 Annual Peter Rabbit wishes you a Very Happy Birthday 8" Plate from *The Tale of Peter Rabbit*. $40.

1983 Annual Peter Rabbit wishes you a Very Happy Birthday 8" Plate Benjamin Bunny and Peter Rabbit from *The Tale of Benjamin Bunny*. $40.

1984 Annual Peter Rabbit wishes you a Very Happy Birthday 8" Plate from *The Tale of Peter Rabbit*. $40.

1982 Annual Peter Rabbit Birthday Plate, Mrs. Tiggy-winkle Wishes You A Very Happy Birthday from *The Tale of Mrs. Tiggy-Winkle*. Note: The only annual birthday plate that does not feature Peter Rabbit. $60.

1985 Annual *Peter Rabbit wishes you a Very Happy Birthday* 8" Plate from *The Tale of Peter Rabbit*. $40.

1989 Annual *Peter Rabbit wishes you a Very Happy Birthday* 8" Plate Peter Rabbit from *The Tale of Benjamin Bunny*. $40.

1986 Annual *Peter Rabbit wishes you a Very Happy Birthday* 8" Plate from *The Tale of Peter Rabbit*. $40.

1990 Annual *Peter Rabbit wishes you a Very Happy Birthday* 8" Plate depicting the February illustration from *Peter Rabbit's Almanac* of 1929. $40.

1991 Annual Peter Rabbit wishes you a Very Happy Birthday 8" Plate. The frontispiece illustration from *Peter Rabbit's Almanac* of 1929. $40.

1992 Annual Peter Rabbit wishes you a Very Happy Birthday 8" Plate. The October illustration from *Peter Rabbit's Almanac* of 1929. $40.

1993 Annual Peter Rabbit wishes you a Very Happy Birthday 8" Plate. The March illustration from *Peter Rabbit's Almanac* of 1929. $40.

1996 Annual Peter Rabbit wishes you a Very Happy Birthday 8" Plate. A repeat illustration from 1991. $30.

1994 Annual Peter Rabbit wishes you a Very Happy Birthday 8" Plate. The front cover illustration of *Peter Rabbit's Almanac* of 1929. $40.

1995 Annual Peter Rabbit wishes you a Very Happy Birthday 8" Plate. Note the new border used from 1995 to 2000 of simple illustrations of carrots, onions and flowers. $30.

1997 Annual Peter Rabbit wishes you a Very Happy Birthday 8"
Plate. A repeat illustration from 1990. $30.

1999 Annual Peter Rabbit wishes you a Very Happy Birthday 8"
Plate. The back cover illustration of *Peter Rabbit's Almanac* of
1929. $30.

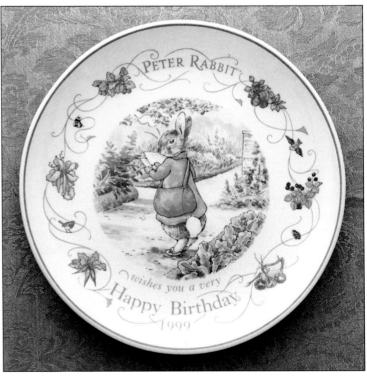

1998 Annual Peter Rabbit wishes you a Very Happy Birthday 8"
Plate from *The Tale of Peter Rabbit*. $30.

2000 Annual Peter Rabbit wishes you a Very Happy Birthday 8" Plate. A repeat illustration from 1992. $30.

2002 Annual Peter Rabbit wishes you a Very Happy Birthday 8" Plate. From *The Tale of The Flopsy Bunnies*. Note the new border design. $30.

2001 Annual Peter Rabbit wishes you a Very Happy Birthday 8" Plate from *The Tale of Mr. Tod*. Note the new border design. $30.

2003 Annual Peter Rabbit wishes you a Very Happy Birthday 8" Plate. From *The Tale of Benjamin Bunny*. This plate is the last in the series. $30.

In 1994, Wedgwood introduced a dated eight inch calendar plate which joined the series of Wedgwood Peter Rabbit annual plates. The calendar plates were issued annually from 1994 through 2002.

1994 Annual Calendar 8" Plate from *The Tale of Peter Rabbit*. $30.

1996 Annual Calendar 8" Plate from *The Tale of Peter Rabbit*. $30.

1995 Annual Calendar 8" Plate from *The Tale of Peter Rabbit*. $30.

1997 Annual Calendar 8" Plate from *The Tale of Peter Rabbit*. $30.

1998 Annual Calendar 8" Plate from *The Tale of Benjamin Bunny*. $30.

1999 Annual Calendar 8" Plate from
The Tale of Benjamin Bunny. $30.

2000 Annual Calendar 8" Plate from March illustration
from *Peter Rabbit's Almanac* of 1929. $30.

2001 Annual Calendar 8" Plate from "The Rabbits Potting Shed," an 1891 illustration. $30.

1993 Peter Rabbit Storybook Mrs. Rabbit etc.... Plaque. $50.

2002 Annual Calendar 8" Plate from *The Tale of Benjamin Bunny*. $30.

In 1993 Wedgwood introduced Peter Rabbit storybook plaques depicting scenes from *The Tale of Peter Rabbit*. These storybook plaques were only out for a very brief time which makes them very collectible today.

1993 Peter Rabbit Storybook Peter Ate Radishes Plaque. $50.

1993 Peter Rabbit Storybook Peter Jumped Plaque. $50.

1993 Peter Rabbit Storybook Bread, Milk & Blackberry Plaque. $50.

1993 Peter Rabbit Storybook Peter Squeezed Under Gate Plaque. $50.

1993 Peter Rabbit Storybook One Spoonful at Bedtime Plaque. $50.

Jasperware

In 1981 Wedgwood introduced an entirely different form of Peter Rabbit giftware. Peter and various members of his immediate family appeared as lifelike figures in white bisque relief on pale blue Jasper. This eight piece Jasperware series included individually boxed a pencil holder, money tray, pill box, egg-shaped box, plate, mini plate, treasure tray and a box. Although it is highly sought after now, in the beginning it was not well received and the collection was retired in 1986.

Blue jasperware

Bone China

In 1981, along with the Jasperware introduction, another different Peter Rabbit series was produced by Wedgwood. Peter Rabbit Bone China miniatures were individually sold in elegant boxes with transparent lids. This series was made up of a tankard, plate, sugar box, tea cup and saucer, teapot, cream jug, coffeepot, and tray. Wedgwood also produced two different illustrations of Peter Rabbit on bone china pendants and six different Beatrix Potter characters each holding their individual books, on bone china thimbles.

Rare Wedgwood Bone China. Originally intended for the Japanese market. Peter and the Red Pocket Handkerchief, copyright 1992, issued in 1993. Teapot 4 ½" high with matching cup and saucer. This representation is from *The Tale of Benjamin Bunny*. Complete Set $500 up.

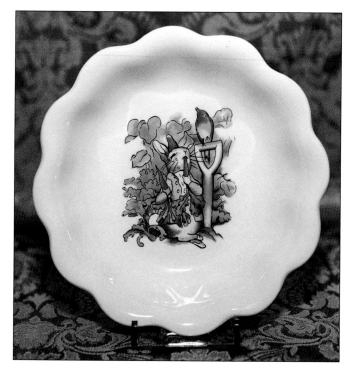

Rare 1962 Wedgwood Bone China Nut Dish with Peter Rabbit motif. $125.

Rare Wedgwood Bone China Bread Plate. Part of the set originally intended for the Japanese market. $250.

Rare Wedgwood Bone China Plate, Oatmeal Bowl and Mug. Part of the set originally intended for the Japanese market. $150 each.

Wedgwood Ornaments

From 1996 through 1999 Wedgwood produced, and offered for sale in the United States, an annual bone china *Peter Rabbit* Christmas ornament: "The Gift", "Two Rabbits Walking", "The Greeting", and "Sleigh Ride". Each ornament coincided with the same illustration on their annual *Peter Rabbit* Christmas plate. These ornaments were made exclusively for collectors in the United States and available in the United States of America only.

Wedgwood Ornament, "Two Rabbits Walking" 1997. Probably a Beatrix Potter design intended for a Christmas card for Hildesheimer & Faulkner, a greeting card publisher. $75.

Wedgwood Ornament, "The Gift," licensed in 1995, issued in 1996. Illustration by Beatrix Potter from the 1894 cover of *Changing Pictures*, a book published by the firm of Ernest Nister. $75.

Wedgwood Ornament, "The Greeting" 1998. One of six Beatrix Potter ca. 1892 illustrations known as "The Rabbits' Christmas Party". $75.

Wedgwood Ornament, "Sleigh Ride" 1999. An early Beatrix Potter ca. 1894 watercolor depicting "Bunnies in the Snow". $75.

Peter Rabbit Nursery Ware
2002 Revised Illustrations

In 2002, Wedgwood created a new series of Peter Rabbit dishes to appeal to younger children. Unfortunately the illustrations are not original Beatrix Potter, and appear more like cartoon figures. The following items are now available in this new design: plate, mug, bowl, snack dish, beaker, moneybox, wall clock, frame, thermometer, a six-piece nursery tea set, and a nine-piece nursery tea set that includes the teapot, sugar, and creamer.

New revised Peter Rabbit Nursery Ware 2002. $60.

New revised Peter Rabbit Nursery Ware; nine piece Childs Tea Set Issued in 2002. Set $100.

Oak Wall Display Case. Houses 24 enameled Crummles covered boxes dating from 1974-1995.
All boxes feature Beatrix Potter characters and each has a value of $200-$300 each.

Oak Wall Display Case. Houses 24 enameled Crummles covered boxes dating from 1974-1995.
All boxes feature Beatrix Potter characters and each has a value of $200-$300 each.

This Oak Wall Display Case Houses the smaller, 1 ½" in diameter, enamel Crummles covered boxes in row two and three. The illustrations on these boxes are a single Beatrix Potter character holding the book he or she was featured in. $150 each.

1982 Biannual Crummles Box Two Bad Mice from *The Tale of Two Bad Mice*. $400.

1986 Biannual Crummles Box Peter Rabbit from *The Tale of Peter Rabbit*. $400.

1984 Biannual Crummles Box Two Bad Mice from *The Tale of Two Bad Mice*. $400.

1988 Biannual Crummles Box Mr. Jeremy Fisher
from *The Tale of Mr. Jeremy Fisher*. $400.

1990 Biannual Crummles Box
Jemima Puddle-duck from *The Tale
of Jemima Puddle-Duck*. $400.

1992 Biannual Crummles Box Mrs. Tiggy-winkle from *The Tale of Mrs. Tiggy-Winkle*. $400.

1993 Peter Rabbit "1893-1993" from *The Tale of Benjamin Bunny*. Limited edition of 500 celebrating Peter Rabbit's Centenary. $400.

1994 Biannual Crummles Box Squirrel Nutkin from *The Tale of Squirrel Nutkin*. Intended to be the last Crummles box issued. $400.

1994 "The Nature of Peter Rabbit" Crummles enamel box. Issued in a limited edition of 100 in conjunction with The Beatrix Potter Society Symposium held in Santa Barbara, California, in August 1994. $400.

Other Crummles Items

Throughout the 1980s into the 1990s, Crummles created numerous Beatrix Potter enamel character items, coinciding with their line of boxes. During the mid 1980s, a series of elaborately illustrated sewing paraphernalia was briefly available featuring the most popular characters. Each item was boxed and sold individually. Seven characters - Peter Rabbit, Jemima Puddle-duck, Mr. Jeremy Fisher, Squirrel Nutkin, Tailor of Gloucester, Mrs. Tiggy-winkle, and Hunca Munca - were available as thimbles, needle cases and as pincushions. Peter Rabbit was briefly available as a tape measure.

Illustrations featuring Peter Rabbit and Jemima Puddle-duck graced two nest egg shaped boxes, and Mr. Jeremy Fisher had his own illustrated frame. Peter and three mice were beautifully illustrated on the lid of an enamel case, which housed a travel clock, with Roman Numerals inside. This illustration was also available as a regular sized enamel box, without the clock. Illustrations and a sentence from The Tale of Peter Rabbit are featured on a Christening napkin ring. The Jemima Puddle-duck coin holder was lavishly illustrated with scenes of Jemima Puddle-duck and the Foxy Whiskered Gentleman. This unique item held pound coins, francs, deutsche marks and dollars.

Enamel Crummles Pincushion $150. Needle Case $200. Thimble $100. All have illustrations from *The Tailor of Gloucester*.

Crummles Christening Napkin Ring 1.5" in diameter c.1980-1990. $125.

Enamel Crummles Pincushion $150. Needle Case $200. Thimble $100. All have illustrations from *The Tale of Squirrel Nutkin*. $150.

87

Enamel Crummles Coin Holder. Illustration from *The Tale of Jemima Puddle-Duck*. $250.

Enamel Crummles Stamp Box. 1994 Bob Smith commission. Illustration from *Cecily Parsley's Nursery Rhymes* and *Appley Dapply's Nursery Rhymes*, Peter Rabbit running around the dome. This stamp box was to be a limited edition of 250, but due to abrupt closure of the company fewer than 80 stamp boxes were created. $300.

Two Egg Shaped Enamel Crummles . Illustrations from *The Tale of Jemima Puddle-Duck* and *The Tale of Peter Rabbit*. $300 each.

Bob Smith Crummles

Bob Smith and his charming English wife, Pat, have been collectors of enamel boxes since the 1960s. Their love of enamel boxes encouraged them to sell their family business and in 1991 begin a new business. Cameron & Smith, Ltd., distributed enamels in the United States concentrating exclusively on and specializing in English Enamels, including those created by Crummles. In 1994 and 1995, Bob was responsible for ten character boxes and a stamp box that he obtained exclusive licensing rights for and had commissioned Crummles to produce. These special character boxes are Little Black Rabbit, Jeremy Fisher Reading Paper, What Time Is It? (the same illustration of the travel clock only smaller with no clock inside), Old Mr. Rabbit Smoking Pipe, and Benjamin Sat on a Bank. Bob also reintroduced, in round shape form, the box "Two Rabbits Under Umbrella" also known as "The Happy Pair." Boxes titled "Tablespoon at Bedtime" and "Peter Posting a Letter" were each issued in limited editions of 250.

Bob also commissioned Crummles to create boxes to be introduced as the first and second annual Christmas Potter boxes, intended to be available in limited editions of 250. The first box featured the illustration Plum Pudding from an 1890 Hildesheimer & Faulkner card and the second box, Rabbit's Party, from the July illustration from *The Peter Rabbit's Almanac of 1929*. Unfortunately Crummles closed their doors before completing the entire 250 editions of each box; therefore only eighty of Plum Pudding and even fewer of the Rabbit's Party were made available.

The commissioned, beautifully illustrated stamp box featured scenes from both *Cecily Parsley's Nursery Rhymes* and *Appley Dapply's Nursery Rhymes* with Peter Rabbit running around the dome. It was to be produced in a limited edition of 150 boxes. Like the Christmas boxes that finished when Crummles & Co., Ltd. closed abruptly, less than eighty stamp boxes were created.

1994-1995 Bob Smith Commissioned Crummles Box "Plum Pudding" from an 1890 Hildesheimer & Faulkner Card. Very Rare, very few were completed. $400 up.

1994-1995 Bob Smith Commissioned Crummles Box "Tablespoon at Bedtime" from *The Tale of Peter Rabbit*. Issued in a Limited Edition of 250. $250.

All of these commissioned enamel boxes are now retired. Bob and Pat Smith, Cameron & Smith, Ltd., continue to be specialists in English enamel boxes and may be contacted through their website: www.cameronsmith.com

1994-1995 Bob Smith Commissioned Crummles Box "Rabbit's Party" from the July 1929 illustration from *Peter Rabbit's Almanac* of 1929. Very Rare, very few completed. $400 up.

Eden—
The Beatrix Potter Collection 1973-2001

Historical Eden

Prior to 1973, in the United States, available licensed Beatrix Potter merchandise consisted mainly of the Frederick Warne books. Also, Beswick figurines and Wedgwood china were imported from England. That all changed in 1973 when The Eden Toy Company of New York was granted a license from Frederick Warne to create a line of Beatrix Potter stuffed characters in plush. Four years later, in 1977, the Schmid Brothers of Randolph, Massachusetts, obtained licensing rights to distribute Beatrix Potter merchandise in many forms such as ceramic music boxes and ornaments. Gift stores soon had their own sections of Beatrix Potter items and more American companies were given licensing rights to produce quality character collectibles. With so many new items to collect, soon various mail order and museum catalogs filled their pages with Beatrix Potter.

It is probably safe to assume that the majority of American collectors of Beatrix Potter own at least one, and more likely several, licensed plush toy Beatrix Potter characters. Serious collectors owe a great deal of thanks to the company Eden Toys Inc., of Jersey City, New Jersey, as they were the first to acquire licensing rights to create Beatrix Potter products in the United States.

In 1939, the Eckstein family of Germany brought their company, Eden, to the United States and began their long and successful career of creating quality and distinctiveness in their creations for young children. In 1965, Richard J. Miller purchased the company. He obtained licensing rights to produce Beatrix Potter characters in 1972. These characters became their first creations. In the spring of 1973, Peter Rabbit, Mr. Jeremy Fisher, and Jemima Puddle-duck were introduced as plush toys to upscale department and toy stores. By the fall of 1973, Tom Kitten, Squirrel Nutkin, Pigling Bland, Hunca Munca, and Benjamin Bunny became available. These well done plush toys became so popular with adults and children alike that, as the years went by, more and more favorite characters were created. Along with the storybook plush characters, Eden become famous for quality musical toys, crib mobiles, infant toys, numerous nursery gifts, and a line of wooden room decor items such as light switch plates, tissue boxes, and foot stools.

Most children receive sometime during their childhood a stuffed Beatrix Potter character, most likely a plush Eden. This is a serious collection of stuffed Eden Peter Rabbits. $100 up each.

Rare Plush Eden characters: Samuel Whiskers, Tailor of Gloucester, Amiable Guinea Pig and Large Samuel Whiskers. $200 up each.

Plush

Soft toy manufacturers sought licensing rights to Beatrix Potter characters since 1909 without success. Finally in the early 1970s, an English company, House of Nisbet, Ltd., was granted exclusive licensing worldwide, with the exceptions of the United States. Cyril Stephens, then Chairman of Frederick Warne & Co., Ltd., authorized the production of a line of high quality, hand made to accurate requirements, Beatrix Potter characters. This line included full size plush characters of Peter Rabbit, Benjamin Bunny, Jemima, Puddle-duck, Tom Kitten, Lady Mouse, Mrs. Tiggy-winkle, and Foxy Whiskered Gentleman. A few characters were also authorized to be produced in miniature. These truly beautifully detailed plush toys were labor intensive. They were produced for only a short time because they were unprofitable to produce based on the cost of labor and material. In 1972, Eden became the exclusive manufacturer of plush Beatrix Potter characters.

Characters and the years they became available

1973 — Peter Rabbit, Mr. Jeremy Fisher, Jemima Puddle-duck, Tom Kitten, Squirrel Nutkin, Pigling Bland, Hunca Munca, Benjamin Bunny

1974 — Mrs. Rabbit, Mrs. Tittlemouse, Foxy Whiskered Gentleman, Mrs. Tiggy-Winkle, Old Mr. Brown, Flopsy, Mopsy & Cottontail, Johnny Town-Mouse, Tabitha Twitchit, Old Mr. Bunny

1975 — Cecily Parsley, Goody Tiptoes, Timmy Tiptoes, Miss Moppet

1976 — Pig Wig, Little Black Rabbit, Lady Mouse

1977 — Sally Henny Penny

1978 — Pickles, Sir Isaac Newton

1982 — Samuel Whiskers, Tailor of Gloucester, Mittens

1984 — Aunt Pettitoes, Amiable Guinea Pig

1988 — Peter Rabbit and Tom Kitten issued as porcelain and plush combined dolls, dressed in velour and available for three years

1990 — Mr. Tod

1992 — Cloth Ginger & Pickles Shop with fabric Peter Rabbit, Benjamin Bunny, Jemima and Sally Henny Penny, Peter Rabbit Hand Puppet

1993 — Tommy Brock

1994 — Mr. McGregor, Gentleman Mouse

1995 — Peter Rabbit, Mrs. Rabbit & Benjamin Bunny debuted for one year as fully jointed characters with plastic medallions

1999/2000 — Peter Rabbit, Jemima Puddle-Duck, Pigling Bland, Tom Kitten, Jeremy Fisher, and Mr. McGregor became available for less than two years as collectible beanbags.

Over the years, Eden also created several highly collectible and today much sought after "special" creations.

For the Christmas season in 1992, Eden issued the Happy Pair; two beautifully dressed fifteen-inch rabbits depicted from Beatrix Potter's famous illustration. In 1993, in honor of Peter Rabbit's 100th anniversary, Eden distributed a very authentic fourteen inch limited edition Peter Rabbit complete with red handkerchief and leather shoes. In 1994, to help celebrate a Monet exhibit held at the Museum of Fine Arts in Boston, Eden produced a limited edition (3000) fourteen inch Peter Rabbit entitled "Master Painter Peter" exclusively for the museum. This Peter Rabbit has moveable arms, legs and head and may be positioned in many poses. In 1995 Eden created another exclusive and limited (500) edition Peter Rabbit for the famous toy store FAO Schwarz. This Peter Rabbit is made entirely of velvet, and holds a radish in his paw.

First Edition 1973 Eden Peter Rabbit from *The Tale of Peter Rabbit*. $200 up.

Eden Tom Kitten, c. 1978 from *The Tale of Tom Kitten*. $100.

Sitting on an antique chair next to her best friend "Jeffy" is an Eden stuffed Hunca Munca from *The Tale of Two Bad Mice* . $50.

Eden 1973, first edition of Benjamin Bunny on left with 1993
version. Both from *The Tale of Benjamin Bunny*. $100 and $85.

Eden 1974, Mrs. Tittlemouse from
The Tale of Mrs. Tittlemouse. $85.

Eden 1974, first
edition of Mrs.
Tiggy-winkle from
*The Tale of Mrs.
Tiggy-Winkle* . $100.

Eden 1974, first edition of Johnny Town-mouse from *The Tale of Johnny Town-Mouse*. In "as is" condition $80 perfect $100.

Eden 1980, 16" Pig-wig. Pig-wig was a tiny black female pig, a breed of black Berkshire pigs, that Beatrix Potter bottle-fed and kept as a household pet. She included Pig-wig as a character in her book; *The Tale of Pigling Bland*. Original sold for $21.95 current value $100.

Eden 1975, first edition of Timmy and Goody Tiptoes from *The Tale of Timmy Tiptoes*. Pair $125.

Eden 1982, Lady Mouse from *The Tailor of Gloucester*. $80.

Eden 1976, first edition of 17" Little Black Rabbit an illustration from *Appley Dapply's Nursery Rhymes*. $75.

Eden first edition 1977, Sally Henny Penny from *The Tale of Ginger and Pickles*. $90.

From *The Tale of Samuel Whiskers*, various Eden versions of Samuel Whiskers, Left to Right: 14"
produced in 1982, center 1991, and 10 ½" Samuel Whiskers produced in 1992. $125, $45, $135.

Variety of Eden Plush Toys; on top shelf, second from left: Tailor of Gloucester 1982
and on top shelf third from left is the 1984 Amiable Guinea Pig. $100 each.

Highly sought after Edens with porcelain heads, hands and feet and plush bodies. $135 each.

1990s Eden Tom Kitten from *The Tale of Tom Kitten*. $60.

Eden 1993, Mr. McGregor from *The Tale of Peter Rabbit* sitting next to a hand made pillow made by Gladys Boalt of Mr. McGregor chasing Peter in his garden. Eden $60. Pillow $50.

Mrs. Tiggy-winkle from *The Tale of Mrs. Tiggy-Winkle* , c.1982. $60.

Eden Tommy Brock from *The Tale of Mr. Tod.* $80.

A later version of an Eden Mrs. Tiggy-winkle, notice not as much detail. $80.

Eden 1991, The Happy Pair. Introduced by Eden for Christmas 1991, priced at $40 each. A beautiful representation in plush of the illustration in Beatrix Potter's booklet called *A Happy Pair* with verses by Frederick E. Weatherly. Pair $200.

A variety of Eden Peter Rabbits from *The Tale of Peter Rabbit*. Left to Right: Peter Rabbits: Exclusive to Neiman Marcus 1990 Peter Rabbit Postman $125. Exclusive to FAO Schwarz 1995 Eden 14" Peter Rabbit covered in velvet from head to toe with pewter buttons fastening his coat. Limited edition of 500. $75. To celebrate Peter Rabbit's 100th birthday in 1993 Eden issued 2,050 Peter Rabbits complete with red handkerchief and shoes. $45. Eden Peter Rabbit issued in 1994 in honor of a Monet exhibit at the Museum of Fine Arts in Boston. Limited edition of 3,000. $65.

Eden Mrs. Rabbit with Flopsy, Mopsy, and Cottontail from
The Tale of Peter Rabbit. Set $350.

Giants

Several characters were created in much larger sizes than the average ten to fifteen inch toy. Originally these "Giant" characters were intended to be store displays but soon became sought after by collectors. In 1974 a thirty-four inch Peter Rabbit became available, followed by an eighteen inch Mrs. Tiggy-winkle, and a thirty-seven inch Mr. Jeremy Fisher. In 1976, a thirty-four inch Mrs. Rabbit and a twenty-three inch Jemima Puddle-duck became available. There were several different Mr. Jeremy Fisher and Peter Rabbit "Giant" versions created during the 1980s.

Giant Eden1992, 35" Peter Rabbit Plush Toy from *The Tale of Peter Rabbit*. $200.

Giant Eden 1974, 37" Mr. Jeremy Fisher Plush Toy from
The Tale of Mr. Jeremy Fisher . $250.

Giant Edens: 1974, 18" Mrs. Tiggy-winkle in the front,
behind her is 1976, 23" Jemima Puddle-duck and next
to her is 1976, 34" Mrs. Rabbit. $200, $150, $150.

Pull Toys

During the years they produced Beatrix Potter characters, Eden created two pull toys: Peter Rabbit and
Jemima Puddle-duck. In 1997 the Peter Rabbit pull toy
was introduced. He wore a blue fleece jacket over a foam
filled body, road on wooden wheels and was pulled by a
twenty-four inch pull cord. Both the Peter Rabbit and
Jemima Puddle-duck pull toys originally sold for twenty-
five dollars.

Musical Toys

Eden was not known for producing musical boxes.
In 1973 they did produce what are called musical waggies
of Peter Rabbit and Jemima Puddle-duck. Over the next
twenty-seven years Eden produced variations of the original Peter Rabbit and Jemima Puddle-duck. When a
waggies is played the characters' head moves. They were
loved by children, but due to their make, were easily
broken. These waggies are highly sought after by collectors and those in perfect to good condition are very valuable. Eden also produced only one known Beatrix Potter character music box; that of Mr. Jeremy Fisher. Today this music box of Mr. Jeremy Fisher is highly collectible.

Hand Puppets

In 1992, Eden produced their only Beatrix Potter
character hand puppet: that of Peter Rabbit. Since it was
the only hand puppet produced, the Eden Peter Rabbit
hand puppet is very rare and highly collectible.

Beanie Babies

Not to be left behind in the beanie baby collectible
craze of the 1990s, Eden introduced three seven inch
character beanies: Peter Rabbit, Jemima Puddle-duck
and Pigling Bland. In 2000, three new characters were
added: Tom Kitten, Mr. Jeremy Fisher and Mr. McGregor.
Of all of the characters, Mr. McGregor became the most
popular thus the most collectible. Originally these five
beanie babies sold for nine dollars each.

Twice yearly in the spring and fall, characters featured in the company catalogs were either added, retired and or altered in appearances. A single character
may have changed appearances several times over the
past twenty-eight years. For example a collector may
possess four completely different designed and sized
Samuel Whiskers. Some characters; Sir Isaac Newt, Pickles, Cecily Parsley, and Old Mr. Brown, were only available for two years. The most popular Eden characters
Peter Rabbit, Benjamin Bunny, Jemima Puddle-Duck,
Mr. Jeremy Fisher, and Tom Kitten have been created in
countless sizes, revisions, and musicals from the 1970s
into the twenty-first century.

During their production, Eden only produced two pull toys: Peter Rabbit and Jemima Puddle-duck. This is the Eden 1997 8" Peter Rabbit Pull Toy. Peter has a blue fleece jacket, over a foam filled body, wooden wheels and 24" pull cord. $75.

This is the Eden Jemima Puddle-duck Pull Toy. $75.

Eden introduced a Peter Rabbit Waggie in 1973. A 10" musical plush whose head moved slowly as music played. Originally sold for $10 but over the next 27 years, various styles emerged with price increases. These "Waggies" were easily broken as they were over loved by children and today they are very rare to find in perfect to good condition. $100.

Highly collectible Mr. Jeremy Fisher with moveable fishing pole, music box in original see through box. Eden is not known for producing music boxes and this was their only one from the Beatrix Potter characters. $250.

Rare and collectible Eden 1992, 12" Peter Rabbit Hand Puppet. The only hand puppet produced by Eden from the Beatrix Potter characters. $200.

Unfortunately, in March 2001, Eden suddenly closed their doors, with no explanation, and have gone out of business. This became quite a shock to retail stores and collectors alike as there was no warning of their closure. This now makes all the creations created and distributed by Eden highly collectible.

Eden Beanie Babies 2000 Mr. McGregor and 1990s Peter Rabbit. Both characters from *The Tale of Peter Rabbit*. $40 each.

Group of Eden Beanie Babies Left to Right: Tom Kitten, Pigling Bland, Mr. Jeremy Fisher. Note: These two slides are the complete Eden set of Beanie Baby Beatrix Potter characters. $40 each.

Schmid —
The Beatrix Potter Collection

Schmid, Inc. History

It is probably safe to assume that today's collector of Beatrix Potter collectibles has a numerous assortment of character items created by the Schmid Company of Randolph, Massachusetts and Toronto, Canada. In fact an individual that collects only Schmid Beatrix Potter items will own an incredibly large and varied collection.

Schmid & Co., was a family owned importing enterprise that started in a basement and was a collaborative effort of Paul A. Schmid and his three sons. They were one of the first companies to introduce moderately priced music boxes in the United States. In 1935 they were also responsible for introducing Hummel figurines from Germany to retailers in the United States. In 1977, Schmid & Co., briefly known as Schmid Brothers, Inc., was granted licensing rights to Beatrix Potter and continued to be a major distributor of quality Potter products until it closed its doors on December 1995. During those eighteen years, Schmid created hundreds of colorful character music boxes, and various ceramic, three dimensional and glass bulb Christmas ornaments, clocks, plagues, resin magnets, tins, flowerpots, nursery ware, pewter items, various types of nightlights, bells, frames, lamps, banks, candleholders, and even a little ceramic village representing various homes of favorite characters.

1977 Schmid Music Box. This is the first Schmid Music Box in the series of Beatrix Potter collectibles. Peter Rabbit Eating Radish from *The Tale of Peter Rabbit* plays "It's a Small World." $125.

1977 Schmid Music Box Mrs. Tittlemouse from *The Tale of Mrs. Tittlemouse* plays "It's a Small World." $200.

1977 Schmid Music Box Mrs. Tiggy-winkle from *The Tale of Mrs. Tiggy-Winkle* plays "Oh What a Beautiful Morning." $200.

1980 Schmid Music Box Duchess from *The Pie and the Patty Pan* plays "Music Box Dancer." $160.

1982 Schmid Music Box Samuel Whiskers from *The Tale of Samuel Whiskers* plays "My Favorite Things." $100.

Schmid Music Boxes, 1977-1995

From 1977 to 1989, Schmid produced music boxes featuring a different Beatrix Potter character on each box. They originally sold for twenty dollars each.

1977 — ten music boxes featuring the following characters: Peter Rabbit, Benjamin Bunny, Jemima Puddleduck, Mr. Jeremy Fisher, Squirrel Nutkin, Tom Kitten, Mrs. Tiggy-winkle, Mrs. Tittlemouse, Tailor of Gloucester, and Pigling Bland.

1978 — Lady Mouse, Squirrel Nutkin, Mr. Tod, and Old Woman in Shoe

1980 — Duchess, Johnny Town-mouse, Miss Moppet, and Mrs. Ribby

1981 — Aunt Pettitoes, Hunca Munca, Amiable Guinea Pig, Sally Henny Penny, Hunca Munca with babies, Little Pig Robinson, and Jeremy Fisher

1982 — Mrs. Rabbit, Mrs. Tabitha Twitchit, Old Mr. Bunny, Goody Tiptoes, and Mrs. Ribby with pitcher. This year all thirty musicboxes were increased in price to $30 each.

1983 — Gentlemen in Snow, Gentlemen in Waiting, Mr. Alderman Tortoise, Cecily, Parsley, Appley Dapply, Samuel Whiskers, and Timmy Willie

1984 — Old Woman in Shoe, Flopsy Bunnies, Pig-wig, Chippy Hackee, Sir Isaac Newton, and Drake Puddle-duck as single character music boxes, the prices increased to $32.50 each. Schmid issued animated musicboxes and the first of many character snowball musicboxes, beginning with Peter Rabbit, for $25 each.

1985 — Poorly Peter, Mrs. Flopsy Bunny, Anna Marie, Simpkin, Rebeccah Puddle-duck, Old Mr. Benjamin Bunny with Peter, John Joiner, Fierce Bad Rabbit, Mrs. Tittlemouse, and Diggory Delvet

1986 to 1988 — Schmid retired some of the original single character musicboxes and increased the price of others to $37.50. A new series of eight revolving music boxes began, which featured an individual character standing on three books with an open book as background. Another series of six character music boxes as snowballs were introduced. Schmid began to produce more giftware, such as assorted character picture frame and mobile ornaments, and mugs, some which were musical.

1989 — four new music boxes featured individual characters revolving on ceramic bases.

Larger character music boxes were also introduced; Peter Rabbit reading, Jemima Puddle-duck reading, The Tailor of Gloucester reading, and Peter Rabbit eating his radishes, all turning as the music played.

Peter Rabbit became available in a large ceramic watering can, moving up and down to the music.

Another series featured eight new music boxes depicting scenes from their individual books, with parts of the scenery revolving. During this time, many of the music boxes were created in Korea and Taiwan.

Schmid introduced a beautiful theme for 1989 Christmas collectibles. Rabbits in the Snow was made in three differently sized music boxes, frames, five different hanging ornaments, a hand painted night light, and a musical relief bell.

A series featured Hunca Munca available as a ten-inch music box and as a seven-inch revolving music box.

1990 — brought an incredible period of growth. A 1994 settlement ended a longstanding battle with the W. Goebal Company of Germany, known for producing Hummel figurines. This helped the Schmid company to emerge from bankruptcy. Sales appeared to be flourishing.

1995 — to the surprise of their customers and 150 employees, Schmid's doors were closed and the company ceased to be one of America's leading giftware distributors.

Beatrix Potter musicals created from 1990-1995

In 1990, Schmid released four ceramic music boxes depicting the homes of Peter Rabbit, Squirrel Nutkin, Tabitha Twitchit and the store of Ginger and Pickles, with the character in sculptured form, revolving in the front. To coincide with the musical village was a large, limited edition of 2,500, detailed music box titled "Benjamin Bunny & Son" which was an open market scene featuring produce with Mr. Bunny and Sally Henny Penny buying and selling goods with Benjamin moving up and down in a barrel.

The Tailor of Gloucester tale was chosen as the delightful theme for an assortment of gifts. The eight-inch music box depicting Simpkin sitting on a stool in front of the china cabinet, with a rotating mouse in the center, was issued in a limited edition of 2,500. Two music boxes shaped as teacups featured Lady Mouse in one and Gentleman Mouse in the other. As the music plays the individual mice rotate. Another music box was shaped as a large teapot, adorned with Lady and Gentleman Mouse. It played "Tea for Two".

During this time, many Schmid collectibles were now being produced in China. Several characters were placed on three-inch-high, paste-colored, plastic-based music boxes with a miniature book in the background. Each character turned as the music played. Peter Rabbit continued to be very popular in his watering can. A smaller version of the 1989 Peter in the watering can music box became available. This representation came in two pieces and played music when turned downward, pretending to pour water. Two garden scenes became available as musicals. One, an individual scene of Peter holding the shovel and carrying a basket, and the other the same scene only depicted as an illustration on the lid of a small round wooden box. For a brief time, Schmid issued a plastic rotating musical cake plate with Peter illustrated in the middle. Peter Rabbit in bed being spoon fed by his mother music box was a great gift for an ill child, and two ceramic egg trinket boxes, one featuring a sculptured Peter Rabbit on top and other featuring Jemima Puddle-duck, played tunes when opened. The 1990 Christmas items included a beautiful, limited edition of 5,000 ceramic Christmas tree music box that featured many characters on and around it with Peter revolving at its base.

In 1991, Schmid released one of their better character themes with music boxes depicting scenes from *The Tale of Two Bad Mice*. The dollhouse, playing the tune "Home Sweet Home", was created and included a front and a back plus an upstairs and downstairs. Furniture is molded to the house and separately a trio of miniature mice may be placed inside. Four individual book scenes made of resin situated on dark wooden bases were available for only one year and are now highly sought after. These delightful musicals depict Hunca Munca and Tom Thumb on the downy bed, sitting at the table trying to carve the ham, avoiding a mousetrap with their babies and spilling the rice from the cabinet.

Two more concept houses as animated music boxes, featuring the homes of J. Dormouse and Timmy Willie,

were introduced. Four musicals were introduced that combined porcelain characters revolving on an oak base. The quartet was made of up of Tabitha Twitchit, Tom Kitten, Benjamin Bunny, and Peter Rabbit. Two unusual musical porcelain baskets became available that featured Peter Rabbit and Jemima Puddle-duck on their handles. These baskets were intended to be used for candy and trinket dishes. At this time, two odd and short termed musicals were distributed featuring Peter Rabbit holding a red cloth bag and another of Jemima Puddle-duck dressed in real fabric bonnet and shawl.

For the Christmas season, Schmid issued a charming set of four detailed music boxes depicting winter rabbits taken from Beatrix Potter's early Christmas cards.

By 1992, Schmid was expanding to include giftware and nursery ware. They temporarily brought back many retired music boxes and kept in stock previously issued music boxes. Four new boxes featured characters in their homes, Mr. Jeremy Fisher reading his paper, Tabitha Twitchit at the fireplace, Mrs. Rabbit at the table with bunnies and Peter coming down the stairs with the onions.

1983 Schmid Music Box Pig-wig from *The Tale of Pigling Bland* plays "Catch a Falling Star." $150.

1983 Schmid Music Box Gentleman in Waiting from *Cecily Parsley's Nursery Rhymes* plays "Tomorrow." $100.

1983 Schmid Music Box Gentleman in Snow from *Appley Dapply's Nursery Rhymes* plays "Try to Remember." $100.

1983 Schmid Music Box Chippy Hackee from *The Tale of Timmy Tiptoes* plays "Feed the Birds." $150.

1985 Schmid Music Box the front of *Ginger and Pickles* from *The Tale of Ginger and Pickles* plays "Top of the World." $300.

1985 Schmid Music Box the back of *Ginger and Pickles* from *The Tale of Ginger and Pickles* plays "Top of the World." $300.

In 1993, Peter Rabbit's centenary was highly celebrated by Schmid with many fine collectibles bearing a marked "100" back-stamp on products limited to 1993 production. The company hosted many parties in upscale gift stores nationwide where attendees could purchase, on that day only, a special three dimensional miniature ceramic ornament of a dated 1993 watering can. Four new music boxes were issued with the new logo. They were: a turning Peter Rabbit coming out of a flowerpot, Peter revolving in front of his book, a colorfully illustrated base with revolving Peter and stationary figures of Benjamin Bunny, Tom Kitten, and Jemima Puddle-duck, and a large Peter in the box, with illustrations on all sides. Peter pops up when played, displaying a mirrored background.

Several new water ball animated character musicals joined the already-existing series. At this time, Schmid introduced a very special musical tarantella of Ginger and Pickles. It is a charming box made of wood and printed paper; when the drawer is open Peter dances to the music.

In 1994, collectors of Schmid products noticed a dramatic downsizing of available products and a lack of new ones. Their Beatrix Potter line once again concentrated on music boxes and a few new different designs of picture frames, rather than on odd giftware. Six of the most popular characters were issued as musicals on bases illustrating the endpapers of the series accompanied by the character's book. Jemima Puddle-

duck and Tom Kitten both joined the series of smaller musical revolving Jack-in-the-Boxes and Jemima Puddle-duck was featured in her own animated tarantella musical box. Two useable musical teapots with removable movements were issued. One was Peter Rabbit in the watering can, and the other was Mrs. Rabbit at the table with her children. Two musical character houses with revolving scenes inside featured Peter at the store of Ginger and Pickles and the other featured Mrs. Rabbit with Peter in their burrow. In 1994, four beautifully illustrated new musical teapots joined the series and were offered at a reduced price: Mr. Jeremy Fisher's house, Simpkin sitting at the cabinet, Hunca Munca's dollhouse, and Peter and Benjamin in front of a house.

Schmid collectibles from 1995 are highly sought after because so few were actually available to collectors. Many new items were offered briefly in mail order catalogs. A new series of darkly painted, revolving, musical characters of Benjamin Bunny, Peter Rabbit, Jemima Puddle-duck, and Mrs. Rabbit were issued at a lower price. New to the series were three musicals featuring the Flopsy Bunnies rotating, a double rotating Mr. Jeremy Fisher, and Mrs. Rabbit with Benjamin Bunny and Peter Rabbit animated. The very last musicals distributed were four water balls of Mr. Jeremy Fisher fishing, Tom Kitten and his sisters at the table, Peter Rabbit and Benjamin Bunny picking onions, and Jemima Puddle-duck with the Foxy Gentleman.

1985 Schmid Music Boxes. Left Benjamin Bunny on Books from *The Tale of Benjamin Bunny* plays "My Favorite Things." $125. Right Peter Rabbit on Books from *The Tale of Peter Rabbit* plays "Peter Cottontail." $125.

1988 Schmid Music Box Peter from *The Tale of Peter Rabbit* plays "I Whistle a Happy Tune." $125.

1989 Schmid Music Box Peter Rabbit in Bed from *The Tale of Peter Rabbit* plays "Spoonful of Sugar." $60.

1989 Schmid Music Box Peter in the Watering Can from *The Tale of Peter Rabbit* plays "Everything is Beautiful." Figurine moves up and down as the music plays. $100.

1989 Schmid Resin Music Box Rabbits in the Snow plays "Winter Wonderland." $150.

1989 Schmid Music Box Rabbits in the Snow plays "Silver Bells." Resin Bell with Lady Rabbit on top. $125.

1990 Schmid Music Box Lady Mouse in Tea Cup from *The Tailor of Gloucester* plays "My Favorite Things." $75.

1990 Schmid Music Box Gentleman Mouse in Tea Cup from *The Tailor of Gloucester* plays "Beautiful Dreamer." $75.

1990 Schmid Music Box a Limited Edition of 2,500. Simpkin at China Cabinet from *The Tailor of Gloucester* plays "On The Street Where You Live." $300.

1990 Schmid Music Box Teapot from *The Tailor of Gloucester* plays "Tea for Two." $150.

1990 Schmid Music Box a Limited Edition of 5,000.
Characters Around the Christmas Tree plays "We Wish You
a Merry Christmas" while Peter Rabbit rotates. $200 up.

1990 Schmid Music Box Peter Rabbit from *The Tale of Benjamin Bunny* plays "Here Comes Peter Cottontail." $120.

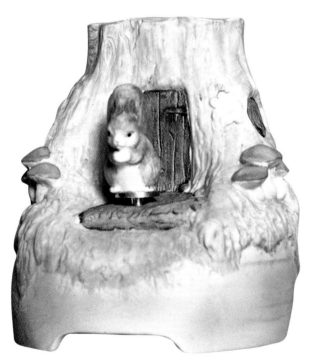

1990 Schmid Music Box Squirrel Nutkin from *The Tale of Squirrel Nutkin* plays "Home Sweet Home." $150.

1990 Schmid Music Box Tabitha Twitchit from *The Tale of Tom Kitten* plays "Lara's Theme." $120.

1990 Schmid Music Box Benjamin Bunny from *The Tale of Benjamin Bunny* plays "My Melody of Love." $120.

1990 Schmid Music Box Tom Kitten from *The Tale of Tom Kitten* plays "My Favorite Things." $120.

Rare, issued only in 1991 Schmid Music Box. Hunca Munca and Tom Thumb on the Downy Bed from *The Tale of Two Bad Mice* plays "Beautiful Dreamer." $150.

116

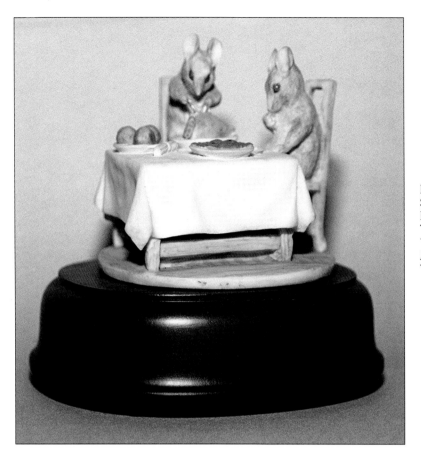

Rare, issued only in 1991 Schmid Music Box. Hunca Munca and Tom Thumb at the table from *The Tale of Two Bad Mice* plays "Close to You." $150.

Rare, issued only in 1991 Schmid Music Box. Hunca Munca with mouse trap from *The Tale of Two Bad Mice* plays "You've Got a Friend." $150.

Rare, issued only in 1991 Schmid Music Box. Hunca Munca spilling the rice from *The Tale of Two Bad Mice* plays "Everything is Beautiful." $150.

1991 Schmid Music Box. Front of The Doll House from *The Tale of Two Bad Mice* plays "Home Sweet Home." $225.

1991 Schmid Music Box. Back of The Doll House from *The Tale of Two Bad Mice* plays "Home Sweet Home." $225.

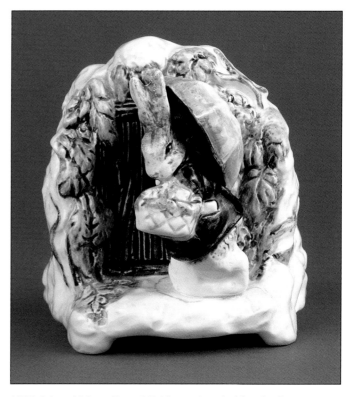

1992 Schmid Music Box of Rabbit at door holding basket with umbrella. A November illustration from *Peter Rabbit's Almanac* of 1929. Plays "Greensleeves." $90.

1992 Schmid Music Box Rabbit at door with bundle of sticks. Illustration from *Peter Rabbit's Almanac* of 1929. Plays "Everything is Beautiful." $90.

1993 Schmid Music Box of Peter Rabbit from *The Tale of Peter Rabbit* in celebration of Peter Rabbit's 100th plays "Here Comes Peter Cottontail." $100.

1993 Schmid Music Box of Rabbit from an early Beatrix Potter illustration plays Chopin's "Nocturne." $90.

1995 The last music box from Schmid. Peter Rabbit eating a radish from *The Tale of Peter Rabbit* plays "Here Comes Peter Cottontail." $80.

Flat Ceramic Ornaments

Beatrix Potter collectors were thrilled to discover, in 1983, six individually wrapped, three-inch high, flat ceramic figurines featuring Peter Rabbit, Benjamin Bunny, Tom Kitten, Mr. Jeremy Fisher, Hunca Munca, and Jemima Puddle-duck as ornaments to decorate their Christmas trees. Initially these ornaments were sold for $6 each. The following year, more characters joined the growing series: Hunca Munca Sweeping, Amiable Guinea Pig, Pigling Bland, Mrs. Ribby, Gentlemen in Snow, Timmy Willie, Sally Henny Penny, Pig-wig, Little Old Woman Who Lived in a Shoe, Drake Puddle-duck, Little Old Woman Knitting, Tailor of Gloucester, Lady Mouse, Poorly Peter Rabbit, Mrs. Flopsy Bunny, Simpkin, Mr. Jackson, Little Black Rabbit, Rebeccah Puddle-duck, Tom Kitten with Butterfly, Aunt Pettitoes, Diggory Delvet, John Joiner, and The Fierce Bad Rabbit.

Nine ornaments became available in 1987, that were more detailed than the lone-figure ornaments. Although still flat, these depicted scenes from individual books: Mrs. Tittlemouse in bed, Peter Rabbit with the spade, Jemima Puddle-duck in front of a gate, Mr. Jeremy Fisher on his lily pad, Tom Kitten with Miss Moppet, Hunca Munca with a pan, Drake Puddle-duck in the garden, Benjamin Bunny holding Peter's shoes, and Mrs. Rabbit with her children.

In time, this series grew to forty, including several dated ones; but by 1988 over half would be retired. The last new flat ornament was issued in 1989, depicting Peter Rabbit in his watering can. Collectors enjoy these delightful ornaments, not only at Christmas but also on Beatrix Potter Easter trees to celebrate the arrival of spring.

1988 Schmid Tin. These tins held the character ornaments that coincided with the picture on the tin. After the ornaments were taken out, these little tins were perfect for holding small treasures such as candy and jewelry. This tin depicts Benjamin Bunny from *The Tale of Benjamin Bunny* and Peter Rabbit from *The Tale of Peter Rabbit*. Tin without ornament $20. Tin with ornament $40.

1988 Schmid Tin. These tins held the character ornaments that coincided with the picture on the tin. After the ornaments were taken out, these little tins were perfect for holding small treasures such as candy and jewelry. This tin depicts Mr. Jeremy Fisher from *The Tale of Jeremy Fisher* and Jemima Puddle-duck from *The Tale of Jemima Puddle-Duck*. Tin without ornament $20. Tin with ornament $40.

Schmid Flat Ceramic Ornament Peter Rabbit in the Watering Can from *The Tale of Peter Rabbit*. $20.

Schmid Flat Ceramic Ornament Peter Rabbit with Radish from *The Tale of Peter Rabbit*. $20.

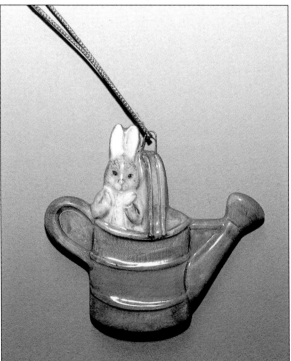

Schmid Flat Ceramic Ornament Benjamin Bunny from *The Tale of Benjamin Bunny*. $20.

Schmid Flat Ceramic Ornament Simpkin from *The Tailor of Gloucester*. $20.

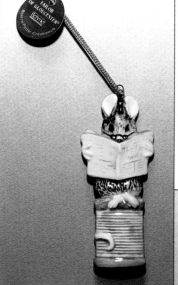

Schmid Flat Ceramic Ornament Tailor of Gloucester from *The Tailor of Gloucester*. $20.

Schmid Flat Ceramic Ornament Poorly Peter from *The Tale of Benjamin Bunny*. $20.

Schmid Flat Ceramic Ornament Mrs. Rabbit from *The Tale of Benjamin Bunny*. $20.

Schmid Flat Ceramic Ornament Lady Mouse from *The Tailor of Gloucester*. $20.

Schmid Flat Ceramic Ornament Hunca Munca with Baby from *The Tale of Two Bad Mice*. $20.

Schmid Flat Ceramic Ornament Mr. Jeremy Fisher from *The Tale of Mr. Jeremy Fisher*. $20.

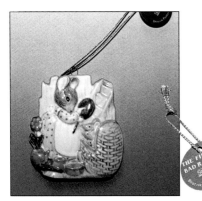

Schmid Flat Ceramic Ornament Hunca Munca from *The Tale of Two Bad Mice*. $20.

Schmid Flat Ceramic Ornament The Good Rabbit and The Bad Rabbit from *The Story of a Fierce Bad Rabbit*. $20.

Schmid Flat Ceramic Ornament Tom Kitten from *The Tale of Tom Kitten*. $20.

Schmid Flat Ceramic Ornament Rebecca Puddle-duck from *The Tale of Tom Kitten*. $20.

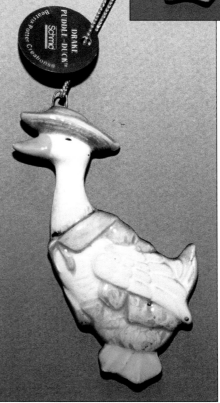

Schmid Flat Ceramic Ornament Mr. Drake Puddle-duck from *The Tale of Tom Kitten*. $20.

Schmid Flat Ceramic Ornament Tom Kitten from *The Tale of Tom Kitten*. $20.

Schmid Flat Ceramic Ornament Mrs. Tittlemouse from *The Tale of Mrs. Tittlemouse*. $20.

Schmid Flat Ceramic Ornament Mr. Drake Puddle-duck from *The Tale of Tom Kitten*. $20.

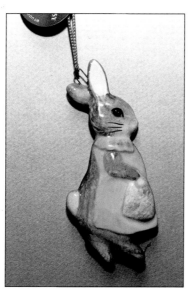

Schmid Flat Ceramic Ornament Jemima Puddle-duck from *The Tale of Jemima Puddle-Duck*. $20.

Schmid Flat Ceramic Ornament Mrs. Flopsy from *The Tale of The Flopsy Bunnies*. $20.

Schmid Flat Ceramic Ornament Sally Henny Penny from *Ginger and Pickles*. $20.

Schmid Flat Ceramic Ornament Mr. Jackson from *The Tale of Mrs. Tittlemouse*. $20.

Schmid Flat Ceramic Ornament Cousin Ribby *from The Tale of Samuel Whiskers or Roly Poly Pudding*. $20.

Schmid Flat Ceramic Ornament Aunt Pettitoes from *The Tale of Pigling Bland*. $20.

Schmid Flat Ceramic Ornament Mouse Knitting from *Appley Dapply's Nursery Rhymes*. $20.

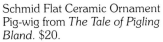

Schmid Flat Ceramic Ornament Pig-wig from *The Tale of Pigling Bland*. $20.

Schmid Flat Ceramic Ornament Little Black Rabbit from *Appley Dapply's Nursery Rhymes*. $20.

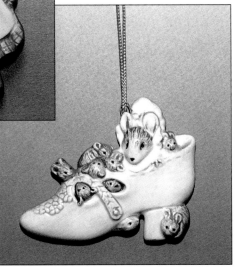

Schmid Flat Ceramic Ornament Old Woman Who Lives in the Shoe from *Appley Dapply's Nursery Rhymes*. $20.

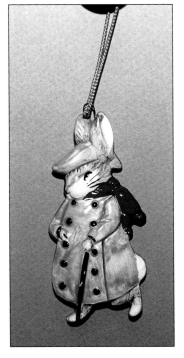

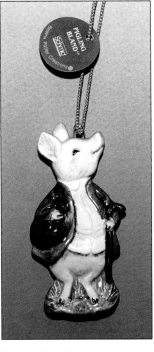

Schmid Flat Ceramic Ornament Pigling Bland from *The Tale of Pigling Bland*. $20.

Schmid Flat Ceramic Ornament Babies First. Not dated. Issued in 1985. $25.

Schmid Flat Ceramic Ornament Gentlemen Rabbit from *Appley Dapply's Nursery Rhymes*. $20.

Schmid Flat Ceramic Ornament Diggory Delvet from *Appley Dapply's Nursery Rhymes*. $20.

Schmid Flat Ceramic Ornament Timmy Willie from *The Tale of Johnny Town-Mouse*. $20.

Schmid Flat Ceramic Ornament Amiable Guinea-pig from *Appley Dapply's Nursery Rhymes*. $20.

Schmid Flat Ceramic Ornament Babies First Christmas Dated 1986. $25.

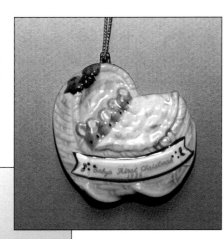

Schmid Flat Ceramic Ornament Babies First Christmas Dated 1988. $25.

Three-dimensional Ornaments

A very successful series of Schmid character ornaments was the miniature three-dimensional (3-D) ceramics. These included, in 1990, Lady Mouse in a Tea Cup, Gentleman Mouse in a Tea Cup, and Lady and Gentleman Mouse in a Teapot from *The Tailor of Gloucester*, and an ornament featuring Peter in Bed. Three different miniature 3-D ornaments, with dates, finalized this series— Peter Rabbit in Watering Can (1993), Peter Rabbit and Benjamin Bunny folding the handkerchief (1994), and Peter Rabbit standing alone (1995).

In 1984, Schmid introduced the first (Peter Rabbit) of their annual boxed 3-D bisque character ornaments for ten dollars. A new character became available for the holidays for the next nine years.

The 1990 Christmas items included; Mr. Jeremy Fisher as the annual 3-D character ornament, a miniature 3-D ornament of Peter in bed being spoon fed. In 1990 three small hanging Christmas ornaments: a teapot, Gentleman Mouse in a teacup, and Lady Mouse in a teacup were introduced.

In 1991, their annual 3-D character ornament was Tom Kitten, and three other new ornaments featured Peter eating his radish on a small hanging plate, a bell, and a ball with its own stand.

In 1991, Schmid introduced four individual hanging bisque Christmas ornaments of the mice from *The Tale of Two Bad Mice*, sitting on a scroll. A line from the story is on each scroll.

In 1992, Tabitha Twitchit was the character for the annual 3-D ornament.

In 1993, Schmid hosted many parties in up-scale gift stores nationwide where attendees could purchase, on that day only, a special 3-D miniature ceramic ornament of a dated 1993 watering can. Lady Mouse became the year's 3-D ornament and six flat ceramic decal

Schmid Flat Ceramic Ornament Babies First Christmas Dated 1987. $25.

ornaments featuring the Tailor of Gloucester, Peter Rabbit, Jemima Puddle-duck, Tom Kitten, Hunca Munca, and Benjamin Bunny, all with ribbons for hanging, were introduced.

In 1994, instead of the usual single annual 3-D character ornament being issued, a completely new series of nine colorful 3-D character ornaments were released, featuring Hunca Munca, Tailor of Gloucester, Sweet Peter, Benjamin Bunny, Tom Kitten, Jemima Puddle-duck, Tabitha Twitchit, Mrs. Rabbit, and Mr. Jeremy Fisher.

The Schmid company closed in 1995 so swiftly and with no warning, so that few gift stores had the opportunity to place their orders; this made many Schmid Beatrix Potter items very rare. The three founding Schmid brothers, John, Paul II, and Alexander, have passed away, but during their lifetimes all gave generously to philanthropic efforts, including to the Schmid Gallery of Chinese Ceramics at the Boston Museum of Fine Arts, which opened in 1989.

Schmid Three Dimensional Ceramic Ornament 1990, Lady and Gentleman Mouse from *The Tailor of Gloucester*. $25.

Schmid Three Dimensional Ceramic Ornament. Rare Peter and The Watering Can promotional store give away to commemorate Peter Rabbits 100th Birthday in 1993. $35.

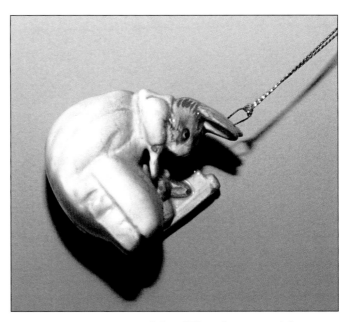

Schmid Three Dimensional Ceramic Ornament 1992, Spooning at Bed Time from *The Tale of Peter Rabbit*. $25.

1990 Schmid Three Dimensional Ceramic Ornaments: Lady Mouse in Tea Cup and Gentleman Mouse in Tea Cup, both from *The Tailor of Gloucester*. $25 each.

ANRI Toriart Figurines

Schmid became the exclusive importer to the United States for ANRI products from Italy. This included the series of twenty, three-inch tall, ANRI Beatrix Potter Toriart character hanging ornaments, priced at $16 each. The series became popular, and in time the same characters became available as mini-ornaments on small, plastic, music boxes and as individual stand-up figurines.

In 1912, in the secluded village of St. Christina high in the Dolomite Mountains of South Tyrol, Italy, a small group of woodcarvers formed a company known as ANRI Woodcarvers. Still existing today, the company creates lovely nativity sets, music boxes, dolls, chess sets and other fine wooden works of art. Each ANRI woodcarving is created from one piece of Alpine maple, that is approximately one hundred years old. In the early 1980s, the Schmid Company of Randolph, Massachusetts, held exclusive distribution rights in the United States to creations of ANRI figurines representing Beatrix Potter characters. For a relatively short period of time, finer gift shops were offering five beautifully hand-carved and hand-painted wooden, Beatrix Potter characters. They were Peter Rabbit holding his radishes, Jemima Puddleduck with ducklings at her feet, Mr. Jeremy Fisher holding his reed pole, Benjamin Bunny holding his onion and handkerchief, and Pigling Bland with his bundle.

ANRI continues to create beautiful creations from wood, but beginning in 1957 and until 1992 the craftsmen at ANRI also used a material they called Toriart to create some molded products. Each Toriart figurine started with a precision-made, hand-carved wooden master model. Using a synthetic resin called Sculptulite, the figurine was molded and meticulously hand-finished and hand-painted. In 1983, ANRI began using Toriart for their new series of licensed Beatrix Potter character hanging ornaments. In the next three years, twenty characters became available, in both three-inch and one-and-a-half-inch high ornaments. In 1985, the same one-and-a-half-inch character hanging ornaments were attached to bases, creating a new collection of standing figurines.

Schmid Three Dimensional Ceramic Ornament 1994, Peter Rabbit and Cousin Benjamin Bunny from *The Tale of Benjamin Bunny*. $40.

Schmid Three Dimensional Ceramic Ornament 1995, Peter Rabbit from *The Tale of Peter Rabbit*. Very Rare Ornament. This is the very last Tale of Peter Rabbit Ornament produced prior to the Schmid Company closing. $50.

Schmid Three Dimensional Annual Christmas Ornament 1985. The first boxed three dimensional resin Christmas Ornament. Peter Rabbit from *The Tale of Peter Rabbit*. $35.

Schmid Three Dimensional Annual Bisque Ornament 1992. Hunca Munca Spilling Rice on Scroll from *The Tale of Two Bad Mice* and Tom Thumb Cutting Ham on Scroll from *The Tale of Two Bad Mice*. $35 each.

Schmid Three Dimensional Annual Bisque Ornament 1992. Hunca Munca on Scroll from *The Tale of Two Bad Mice* and Tom Thumb and Baby Mouse on Scroll from *The Tale of Two Bad Mice*. $35 each.

Schmid Plate 3 ¼" diameter Ornament 1989, with early Beatrix Potter illustration from Rabbits in the Snow. $35.

1989 Rare Schmid Ceramic Ornament, "Our First Christmas Together" from the illustration "Rabbits in the Snow." $35.

1990 Rare Schmid Ceramic Ornament, "Happy Anniversary" from The Tail of Peter Rabbit. $35.

Schmid Three Dimensional Ornament. One of four resin characters that came in a tin with magnet. This is Peter Rabbit from *The Tale of Peter Rabbit*. $20.

Schmid Plate 3 ¼" diameter Ornament 1990, Peter Rabbit in Garden from *The Tale of Peter Rabbit*. Intended to be the beginning of annual plate ornament series, which were never produced. $35.

Rare Schmid Centenary Ornament, 1993 production only, Peter Rabbit from *The Tale of Peter Rabbit*. $40.

Schmid Character Book Ornament, *The Tale of Mr. Jeremy Fisher*. $25.

Schmid Character Book Ornament, *The Tale of Jemima Puddle-Duck*. $25.

The following characters were available in Toriart, in both sizes of hanging ornaments and the one-and-a-half-inch standing figurines:
Peter Rabbit
Old Mr. Bunny
Benjamin Bunny
Little Pig Robinson
Jemima Puddle-duck
Mrs. Tiggy-winkle
Mr. Jeremy Fisher
Tailor of Gloucester
Pigling Bland
Miss Moppet
Tom Kitten
Johnny Town-mouse
Hunca Munca
Old Mr. Brown
Mrs. Rabbit
Sally Henny Penny
Mr. Tod
Amiable Guinea Pig
Timmy Tiptoes
Mrs. Ribby

Shortly after the Toriart standing figurines were introduced, ANRI began a series of music boxes, utilizing the same Beatrix Potter Toriart character figurines on resin and plastic bases, which contained the Swiss-made musical implements. Collectors should know that only fourteen of the original series of twenty Toriart figurines were ever available in music box form. The entire Beatrix Potter ANRI Toriart Beatrix Potter collection retired in 1991. While the five wooden ANRI hand-carved figurines are extremely rare, and difficult to find today, the ANRI Toriart collection of figurines, including music boxes, has been easier to locate through the Internet, and often is priced considerably less than the original prices.

1985 ANRI Toriart Music Boxes. Right Tom Kitten from *The Tale of Tom Kitten* plays "Brahm's Lullaby". Left Mrs. Tiggy-winkle from *The Tale of Mrs. Tiggy-Winkle* plays "Brahm's Lullaby." $75 each.

1985 ANRI Toriart Music Boxes. Right Peter Rabbit from *The Tale of Peter Rabbit* plays "Minuet Bach". Left Benjamin Bunny from *The Tale of Benjamin Bunny* plays "Minuet Mozart." $75 each.

1986 ANRI Toriart Music Boxes. Right Mrs. Ribby from *The Tale of the Pie and the Patty Pan* plays "Memory." Left Tailor of Gloucester plays Chopin's "Nocturne." $75 each.

Toriart Figurines: 3" and 1 ½" Gentleman in the Snow from *Appley Dapply's Nursery Rhymes*. $45 each.

Toriart Figurines: 3" and 1 ½" Peter Rabbit from *The Tale of Peter Rabbit*. $45 each.

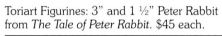

Toriart Figurines: 3" and 1 ½" Tom Kitten
from *The Tale of Tom Kitten*. $45 each.

Toriart Figurines: 3" and 1 ½" Johnny Town-mouse from *The Tale of Johnny Town-Mouse*. $45 each.

Toriart Figurines: 3" and 1 ½" Benjamin Bunny from *The Tale of Benjamin Bunny*. $45 each.

Toriart Figurines: 3" and 1 ½" Tailor of Gloucester from *The Tailor of Gloucester*. $45 each.

Border Fine Arts Figurines

1989 was the most prolific for new Beatrix Potter merchandise. Schmid became the sole distributor, in the United States of America, of the finely detailed, handcrafted Beatrix Potter figurines from a Scottish company, Border Fine Arts. Fifteen figurines, housed in colorfully illustrated tins, were immediately well received by collectors.

Border Fine Arts, finely detailed, handcrafted Beatrix Potter Peter Rabbit figurine, housed in colorfully illustrated tin. $200.

Very Rare ANRI wood carvings of Mr. Jeremy Fisher, Jemima Puddle-duck, Benjamin Bunny, Pigland Bland and Peter Rabbit. These beautiful wood carvings are carved out of one piece of alpine maple. $300 up.

Border Fine Arts, Christmas Tree Limited edition. $300 up.

Border Fine Arts, *Ginger and Pickles*. $400 up.

Border Fine Arts, Peter Rabbit in the Garden. $400 up.

Other Beatrix
Potter Character Collectibles

Steiff, 19th to 21st Century

The Steiff Company is the oldest toy stuffed animal manufacturer in the world. In 1890 a German seamstress, Margarete Steiff, began hand-crafting toy animals using the finest materials and taking up to thirty sections of fur fabric for each animal. Every Steiff tuffed animal is identified by a button in the toy's ear. Until 1900, Steiff used an elephant with an "s" shaped trunk as a business logo (an elephant was the first animal Maragrete Steiff created). Many companies tried to imitate Maragrete Steiff's creations, and it was these imitations that inspired her to design a more permanent and recognizable trademark. Since 1904, Steiff has used a small black button in the left ear of each of its toy stuffed animals. Based on the ruling of the German patent office, the button is not what is registered, but it is the words "button-in-the-ear," in German "knopf im ohr," that are protected.

In 1905, Steiff produced a Peter Rabbit toy emulated from Beatrix Potter's tales. This rabbit wears a felt jacket and slippers and was marketed by Steiff, not as Peter Rabbit but as a "rabbit with a blue jacket." The rabbit was sold at Harrods Department Store in London and the tag stated "Hase aufwartend mit Frack." These Steiff rabbits are extremely rare and valuable today, and if found cost well over five thousand dollars. In 2002, Steiff created a Peter Rabbit celebrating his one-hundredth birthday. These rabbits are available on the secondary market today for around five hundred dollars.

Very Rare Steiff Rabbit, c. 1905. Sold by Steiff not as a Peter Rabbit, but as a Rabbit with a blue jacket. Sold at Harrods with the tag stating: "Hase aufwartend mit Frack," loosely translated means "Farmer Rabbit in dress." $5,000 up.

Three Steiff Peter
Rabbits. $125 up.

Steiff Peter Rabbit in Commemoration with Peter
Rabbits 100th Birthday Celebration. $125.

Huntley & Palmer's Biscuit Tins

Many collectors of Beatrix Potter collectibles own round tins that feature a colorful illustration of a Beatrix Potter character and the words "Huntley & Palmers Biscuits" etched on the rim. These tins originally kept bakery goods from this English company fresh.

As a young baker, Joseph Huntley started his small shop on London Street in Reading, England, in 1822. George Palmer became his partner in 1841, and in just a few years their shop became a factory large enough to be thought of as a town, soon to be known the world over as "Biscuit Town."

In 1832, Joseph Huntley's son, Joseph, began making tin boxes in his ironmonger's shop specifically for his father's biscuits. His tins provided a major advantage to Huntley & Palmer over other food exporters; for they ensured that the biscuits inside stayed airtight, oven-fresh, and unbroken, sometimes for years as they traveled with sailors to distant customers around the world. The tins themselves, in different shapes and sizes, and with various logos, became highly prized as well as the biscuits inside.

By 1900, Huntley & Palmer was the largest biscuit manufacturer in the world, employing 5,000 men and woman in factories that covered 24 acres of land. They produced over 400 different biscuit varieties along with cakes and other treats. Huntley & Palmer remained an active bakery for 150 years until 1982 when Nabisco purchased the company. Today, the company no longer exists but the Museum of Reading, England, is home to over 300 Huntley & Palmers' biscuit tins beginning with its first printed creation in 1868. Beatrix Potter collectors will be interested in knowing that there were several character tins created by Huntley & Palmers that featured colorful Beatrix Potter character illustrations on their lids.

Huntley and Palmer Tin 1974-1978, Peter Rabbit in the Garden from *The Tale of Peter Rabbit*. $45.

Rare 1955 Huntley and Palmer Tin of Mrs. Tittlemouse from *The Tale of Mrs. Tittlemouse*. $75.

Huntley and Palmer Tin 1974-1978, Mr. Jeremy Fisher from *The Tale of Mr. Jeremy Fisher*. $45.

138

Huntley and Palmer Tin 1974-1978, Jemima Puddle-duck and Foxy Whiskered Gentleman from *The Tale of Jemima Puddle-Duck*. $45.

Huntley and Palmer Tin 1974-1978, Mrs. Tiggy-winkle from *The Tale of Mrs. Tiggy-Winkle*. $30.

Huntley and Palmer Tin 1974-1978, Tom Kitten from *The Tale of Tom Kitten*. $45.

12" Tin Flopsy, Mopsy and Cottontail around the black berry bowl from *The Tale of Peter Rabbit*. $45.

12" Tin Mrs. Rabbit, Flopsy, Mopsy and Cottontail from
The Tale of Benjamin Bunny. $45.

12" Tin Compilation of Beatrix Potter Characters
created in 1924 by Beatrix Potter as a section of a card
for the Invalid Children's Aid Association named "Peter
and his friends need your help!" $45.

12" Tin Peter Rabbit and Family from
The Tale of Peter Rabbit. $45.

1986 Made in England, Hunkydory 13 ½" Tin Tray featuring Peter Rabbit and characters. $45.

Rare Antique Tin, c. 1935 illustration from *The Tale of Peter Rabbit*. $150 up.

Rare Antique Tin, c. 1935 illustration from *The Tale of Peter Rabbit*. $150 up.

Rare Antique Tin, c. 1935 illustration from *The Tale of Peter Rabbit*. $150 up.

Rare, Antique Biscuit Tin front and back. Made by Huntley, Boorne & Stevens for McVitie & Price, Edinburgh in 1939. $400 up.

Teleflora

In 1996 Teleflora, the world's largest privately owned floral wire service, received licensing rights to produce Peter Rabbit designs as part of their "Flowers in a Keepsake Gift" spring promotion. The first "gift" was a beautifully illustrated canister with lid. It was so well received that Teleflora continued their popular Peter Rabbit theme every spring with a different illustrated canister, until the last one was issued in 2004.

1998 Teleflora Peter Rabbit Wicker Baskets. $15 each.

1997 Teleflora Peter Rabbit Flowerpot with sculptured Peter Rabbit attached to side of pot. $25.

McDonald's

McDonald's Peter Rabbit Happy Meal was a 1988 promotion for the Northeast only, including New York, for one month. During that one month, over one million were sold. Four different Tales could be purchased in the Peter Rabbit Happy Meal Box: *The Tale of Peter Rabbit, The Tale of Benjamin Bunny, The Tale of Squirrel Nutkin,* and *The Tale of the Flopsy Bunnies.* Each of the McDonald's books carried the McDonald's seal on the book cover.

Toy Works

The Toy Works Inc., in New York state, was established in 1973 as a small company to create silk-screened textile products for the gift industry. They received licensing rights for Beatrix Potter in the mid-1980s and throughout the decade of the 1990s, created and distributed a varied collection of fun and useful giftware featuring Potter characters. Tote bags, backpacks and lunch bags made excellent gifts for collectors of all ages. For the home The Toy Works handcrafted rugs, pillows, draft stoppers, doormats and doorstops featuring not only lone Beatrix Potter characters but also collectibles with more than one character and/or scenes. For children Toy Works Inc., distributed colorfully illustrated cloth chime balls, books and a very sweet series of finger puppets.

C & F Enterprise

C&F Enterprise were distributors only, but responsible for distributing many Beatrix Potter characters to better gift shops all over the United States.

Mattel

Mattel offered two Barbie dolls with Beatrix Potter characters on their dresses. The first, Keepsake Treasure Barbie, was issued in 1998. She was dressed in a coral satin dress with puffed sleeves and an ivory skirt decorated with Beatrix Potter characters. The second was issued in 2002 as a commemorative Barbie, for Peter Rabbit's one-hundredth birthday celebration. She was dressed in a blue dress decorated with Beatrix Potter characters.

Jamestown Mint

Jamestown Mint introduced a Peter Rabbit ornament in 1995. Jamestown Mint had intended a series of Beatrix Potter characters to be an annual ornament available through mail order but, after the initial Peter Rabbit ornament was introduced, the line was discontinued.

McDonald's Happy Meal Front and Back of Box and Book. 1988 promotion for the Northeast only. $45.

The Toy Works 1989 Cloth Christmas Stocking Merry Christmas from Peter Rabbit. $25.

1999 C & F Enterprise Christmas Pillow. $60.

The Toy Works 1989 Cloth Christmas Stocking Merry Christmas from Peter Rabbit. $25.

The Toy Works 1989 Cloth Christmas Stocking Merry Christmas from Peter Rabbit. $25.

1999 C & F Enterprise Christmas Stocking. $50.

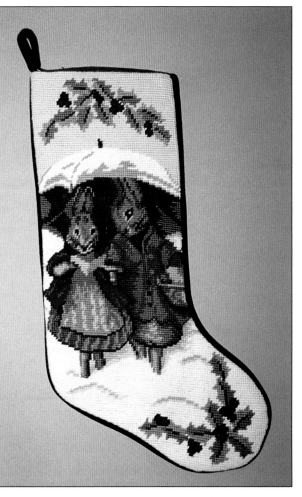

1999 C & F Enterprise Christmas Stocking. $50.

1999 C & F Enterprise
Christmas Stocking. $50.

Wonderful Christmas tree covered with Original Creations in front of a large collection of Peter Rabbits, all on top of a Toy Works rug. Rug $175.

1995 Jamestown Mint Peter Rabbit ornament. Available for one year only then the line was discontinued. $15.

1997 Mattel, Barbie Doll in original box. $60.

Original Creations

Gladys Boalt Ornaments

New Yorker Gladys Boalt has been creating detailed, soft-sculpture character ornaments on muslin for over twenty-five years. They are prized possessions of individuals who collect items featuring their favorite childhood storybook characters, historical heroes, animals, etc. Her exquisite decorations have even graced the White House Christmas tree.

Because of their fine details, Boalt's creations are not mass-produced or widely available, but are highly sought after. A small group of talented seamstresses work on various parts of each ornament. A single, entirely handmade, ornament can involve as many as forty plus different steps, including the fashioning of heads, bodies, feet, and clothing before it is ready for Ms. Boalt to create the faces and sign and date each finished ornament.

During the 1980s, Gladys Boalt added several Beatrix Potter characters to her growing business of creating handmade decorations, pillows, and quilts. The following list includes just a few of her Potter ornament representations and the year they were first issued: Peter Rabbit (1986), Benjamin Bunny (1986), Tabitha Twitchit (1986), Duchess (1987), Mrs. Rabbit (1987), Ribby (1987), Tom Kitten (1987), Old Mr. Benjamin Bunny (1987), Mrs. Tiggy-winkle (1988), and Jemima Puddle-duck (1988).

Gladys Boalt Original 1986, Peter Rabbit and Mrs. Rabbit from *The Tale of Peter Rabbit*. $60 each.

Gladys Boalt Original 1987, Tom Kitten and Tabitha Twitchit from *The Tale of Tom Kitten*. $60 each.

Gladys Boalt Original 1987, Duchess and Mrs. Ribby from *The Tale of The Pie and The Patty Pan*. $60 each.

Gladys Boalt Original 1987, Benjamin Bunny and Old Mr. Bouncer from *The Tale of Benjamin Bunny*. $60 each.

Gladys Boalt Original 1988, Jemima Puddle-duck from *The Tale of Jemima Puddle-Duck* and Mrs. Tiggy-winkle from *The Tale of Mrs. Tiggy-Winkle* . $60 each.

R. John Wright

Doll collectors nationwide rejoiced when R. John Wright Dolls, Inc. announced, in 1998, that they had obtained the licensing rights to create a series of exquisite, hand-made, mohair plush, Beatrix Potter characters. R. John Wright, Inc. created their first doll in 1976, and over the next two decades established itself as one of the leading doll manufacturers in the world. Among the many awards bestowed on this company, located in Bennington, Vermont, are the Doll of the Year (DOTY) Award, the Golden Teddy Award, and the Dolls Magazine Award of Excellence. The company already had an enormous following of Winnie-the-Pooh collectors. In 1998, Beatrix Potter collectors gleefully look forward to obtaining their favorite characters in custom-woven mohair plush creations, with detailed features and glass eyes. Peter Rabbit, wearing his famous blue jacket complete with brass buttons and holding a radish, premiered in 2000 in a limited edition of 2,500. Jemima Puddle-duck followed him the following year, in a limited edition of 1,500.

In 2005, R. John Wright's "Beatrix Potter Collection" consists of ten handmade characters that include Benjamin Bunny, Jemima's Ducklings, and Tom Kitten. More favorite characters are scheduled for creation in the near future.

A collection of R. John Wright Originals. Left to Right: Jemima Puddle-duck, Benjamin Bunny, Peter Rabbit, Peter Rabbit gardening, Tom Kitten, A Flopsy Bunny. $600-$800 up each.

Gina Hart

Many collectors not only love but are passionate about the Beatrix Potter characters and illustrations. A few collectors with artistic talent have chosen to make their own special creations of Beatrix Potter's characters. For example, Gina Hart, and English artist, paints in painfully exquisite detail using an eyelash.

R. John Wright Tom Kitten from *The Tale of Tom Kitten*. $600 up.

1998 Gina Hart Original Hand Painted Version of Tom Kitten from *The Tale of Tom Kitten*. Note the exquisite detail and the fact that this is all hand painted using eye lashes.

2001 Gina Hart Original Hand Painted compilation of characters from *The Tale of Tom Kitten* and *The Story of a Fierce Bad Rabbit* in front of Hill Top. Note the exquisite detail and the fact that this is all hand painted using eye lashes for the flowers.

Linda Long

Linda Long's creations are hand made, without a pattern, and every detail is hand stitched.

Linda Long Original, Peter Rabbit Post Man from *Peter Rabbit's Almanac* for 1929. $100-$200.

Linda Long Original, Peter Rabbit from *The Tale of Peter Rabbit*. $100-$200.

Linda Long Original, Mrs. Rabbit from *The Tale of Peter Rabbit*. $100-$200.

150

Linda Long Original, Gentlemen in the Snow from
Appley Dapply's Nursery Rhymes. $100-$200.

Linda Long Original,
Little Black Rabbit. $100-
$200.

Linda Long Original, Benjamin
Bunny from *The Tale of Benjamin
Bunny*. $100-$200.

Miriah Champaign

Miriah Champaign makes charming felt Christmas ornaments.

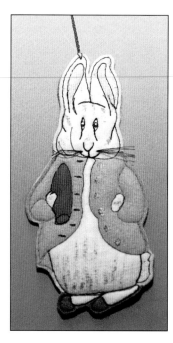

Miriah Champaign Original, Peter Rabbit from *The Tale of Peter Rabbit*.

Miriah Champaign Original, Pigling Bland from *The Tale of Pigling Bland*.

Miriah Champaign Original, Jemima Puddle-duck from *The Tale of Jemima Puddle-Duck*.

Miriah Champaign Original, Benjamin Bunny from *The Tale of Benjamin Bunny*.

Miriah Champaign Original, Mouse Knitting.

Jennifer Reed Original Kit Stocking "Kara." $20 in kit form.

Miriah Champaign Original, Mr. Jeremy Fisher from *The Tale of Mr. Jeremy Fisher*.

Miriah Champaign Original, Tom Kitten from *The Tale of Tom Kitten*.

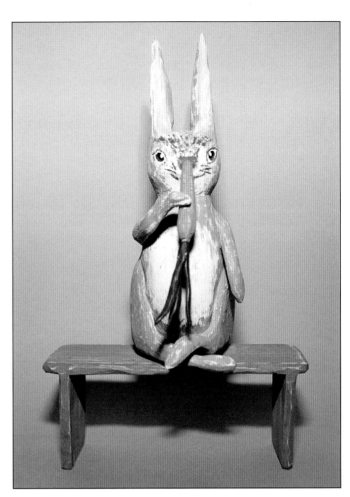

John Sewall Original 1995, Fierce Bad Rabbit from *The Story of a Fierce Bad Rabbit*.

Miriah Champaign Original, Johnny Town-mouse from *The Tale of Johnny Town-Mouse*.

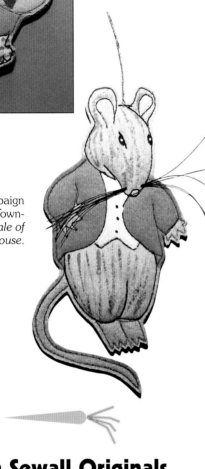

John Sewall Originals

John Sewall has created a garden with hand carved wooden characters placed among the flower beds (exactly as Beatrix Potter illustrated them in her *Tales*). Annually, he hand-carves a character, with the exact detail seen in the appropriate Beatrix Potter illustration, to give as a surprise Christmas gift to his beloved wife, Kara. We would never presume to claim that we know what Beatrix Potter would think, but who wouldn't be proud of this highest form of compliment.

John Sewall Original 1993, Benjamin Bunny from *The Tale of Benjamin Bunny*.

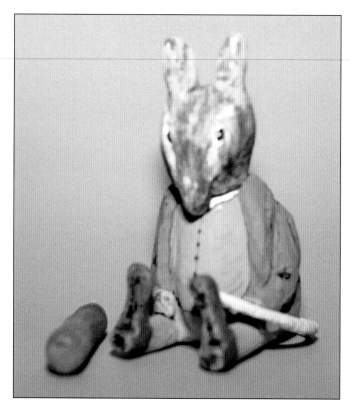

John Sewall Original 1996, Samuel Wishers from
The Tale of Samuel Whiskers or *Roly Poly Pudding*.

John Sewall Original 1998, Simpkin
from *The Tailor of Gloucester*.

John Sewall Original 1999, Flopsy Bunnies from
The Tale of The Flopsy Bunnies.

John Sewall Original 1997, Tom Kitten
from *The Tale of Tom Kitten*.

John Sewall Original 2000, Timmy Willie in The
Pea Pod from *The Tale of Johnny Town-Mouse*.

John Sewall Original 2001, Mrs. Tiggy-winkle
from *The Tale of Mrs. Tiggy-Winkle*.

John Sewall Original 2000, Timmy Under Strawberry
Leaf from *The Tale of Johnny Town-Mouse*.

John Sewall Original 2004, Guinea Pig Gardener from *Cecily Parsley's Nursery Rhymes*.

John Sewall Original 2002, The Tailor of Gloucester from *The Tailor of Gloucester*.

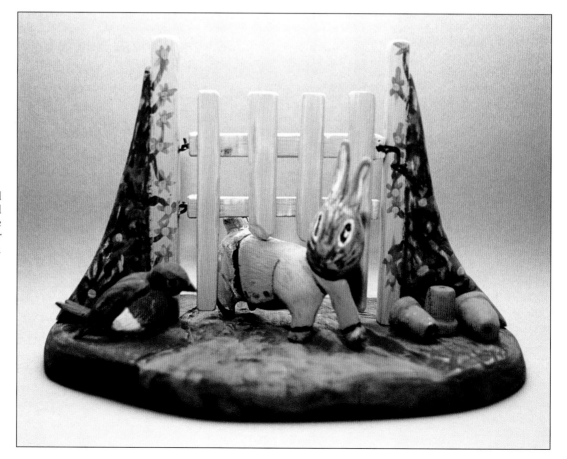

John Sewall Original 2003, Peter Rabbit and Mr. McGregor's Fence from *The Tale of Peter Rabbit*.

Collection of John Sewall Originals.

Collection of John
Sewall Originals.

Collection of John Sewall Originals.

The Beatrix Potter Society

Students, collectors, fans, and enthusiasts have been able to keep up with the always interesting world of Beatrix Potter by belonging to the Beatrix Potter Society. A small group of individuals, professionally involved with Beatrix Potter, formed the Society in England in 1980. It has a worldwide membership of over 900 members currently, who eagerly await the arrival of four, extremely informative newsletters that arrive quarterly. Every two years the Society hosts an International Study Conference that features guest speakers, tours, and interesting discussions that pertain to Beatrix Potter and her works. Thespeakers' talks are published in book form in the series *Beatrix Potter Studies*. The *Studies* now number eleven volumes, and each one includes a wealth of information not found in any other publication. This society brings together individuals of varied backgrounds who share the same wonderful interest—Beatrix Potter. Throughout the United States, Beatrix Potter Society members create special gatherings, many times coinciding with a Beatrix Potter exhibit or event.

The Beatrix Potter Society protects the integrity and work of Beatrix Potter and uses some of its funds to assist Potter-related projects, such as improvements to the farms and other lands she willed to the National Trust and to the care and protection of her watercolors.

The society welcomes new members from the world over, and has liaison officers in the United States, Australia, and Japan. For more detailed information regarding the Beatrix Potter Society, please send inquiries to: The Beatrix Potter Society, 9 Broadfields, Harpenden, Herts AL5 2HJ, UK
or visit info@beatrixpottersociety.org.uk.

Bibliography

Batkin, Maureen. Gifts for Good Children, The History of Children's China Part II, 1890-1990. Richard Dennis, Great Britain, 1990.

Dale, Jean. Storybook Figurines, Royal Doulton, Royal Albert, Beswick. Ontario, Canada: Charlton International Inc., 2004.

Hobbs, Anne Stevenson. Beatrix Potter's Art. London: Frederick Warne, 1989.

Hobbs, Anne Stevenson and Whalley, Joyce Irene. Beatrix Potter: The V & A Collection. London: The Victoria & Albert Museum and Frederick Warne, 1985.

Irvine, Louise. John Beswick & Royal Albert Beatrix Potter Figures. UK International Ceramics, 1992.

Lane, Margaret . The Tale of Beatrix Potter. London: Frederick Warne, 1946; revised edition 1968.

Lane, Margaret. The Magic Years of Beatrix Potter. London: Frederick Warne, 1978.

Linder, Leslie. The Art of Beatrix Potter. London: Frederick Warne, 1955; revised edition,1972.

Linder, Leslie. A History of the Writings of Beatrix Potter. London: Frederick Warne, 1971; revised edition, 1987.

Potter, Beatrix. The Complete Tales of Beatrix Potter. London: Frederick Warne, 1989.

Sweet, Marilyn. The Charlton Standard Catalogue of Border Fine Arts and Storybook Figurines. Ontario, Canada: Charlton International Inc., 2000.

Taylor, Judy. Beatrix Potter: Artist, Storyteller and Countrywoman. London; Frederick Warne, 1986; revised edition, 2002.

Taylor, Judy. That Naughty Rabbit. London: Frederick Warne, 1987; revised edition, 2002.

Taylor, Judy. Beatrix Potter's Letters. London: Frederick Warne, 1989; revised edition, 2002.

Taylor, Judy. Letters to Children from Beatrix Potter. London: Frederick Warne, 1992; revised edition, 2002.

Taylor, Judy. So Shall I Tell You a Story. London: Frederick Warne, 1993.

Taylor, Judy, Whalley, Joyce Irene, Hobbs, Anne Stevenson and Battrick, Elizabeth M. Beatrix Potter 1866-1943: The Artist and Her World. London: Frederick Warne and the National Trust, 1987; revised edition, 1995.